Scents of
the Soul

Creating Herbal Incense for
Body, Mind and Spirit

Scents of the Soul

Creating Herbal Incense for Body, Mind and Spirit

Ginger Quinlan

FINDHORN PRESS

Published in 2009 by Findhorn Press, Scotland

ISBN 978-1-84409-174-4

Edited by Michael Hawkins
Cover design by Damian Keenan
Interior design by Damian Keenan

Printed and bound in the US

1 2 3 4 5 6 7 8 9 10 11 12 14 13 12 11 10 09

Published by
Findhorn Press
305a The Park, Findhorn
Forres IV36 3TE
Scotland, UK

Telephone
+44-(0)1309-690582
Fax
+44-(0)131-777-2177
info@findhornpress.com
www.findhornpress.com

Contents

Contents

About the Author

INTUITION has always been a part of my life. At a very early age, ten to be exact, I became aware of the fact that I was "different" from other little girls. I saw things that were not visible to others. I knew and felt things before they happened, things that my parents preferred not to recognize.

My life was not a normal existence but one filled with spirits, energy and *knowing* what one should not know at such an early age.

When I turned 15 the drive to find out why I was so different kicked in. It sent me on a search through countless library books, endless discussions with my youth Pastor at the Baptist Church we belonged to and fruitless efforts to find information about why I felt, saw and experienced things before they happened. This led to discovering a wide variety of paths that seemed to all lead me back to being one with Mother Earth and all She had to offer.

During this time of self-discovery, my Father, a gracious man who spent all of his free time digging in the dirt behind our home, took me under his kindly wings, introducing me to the world of plants, hybridizing and breeding Iris especially. I was a willing, delighted student, happy to spend quality time with the man who was my hero. I dug side by side with him every weekend, planting rows and rows of crinkled looking Iris bulbs.

I loved the way the dirt lingered between my toes while I bent over the Iris, plucking tiny seed pods from their middles, then carefully labeling them and plopping them in tiny brown paper bags for later use. I couldn't find a happier time than working the garden, feeling the spring sun beaming down all around us as we dug in the rich dirt of my backyard. My father's passion became my own.

Gardening, along with all the nature studies, drew me into its bountiful array of healing modalities. I dedicated my early years to studying, growing and drying herbs, working with essential oils from plants, experimenting with the effects of herbs and oils on the human body, energy movement and manifestation work. In between my studies, I was becoming a very well known Psychic-Medium. My life became a dance of playing in the ethers during my normal working week, and playing in the dirt, in my free time to discover the benefits of healing with herbs.

Herbs are my friends. They grow, they prosper, they make me smile and they are always honest about what they need and who they are. This combination of gardening and working with energy on a daily basis brought me to a complete halt in my studies and work.

The more I searched for information about healing with color, energy, breath and other tools to manifest change in one's life, the less I found. I bought numerous manuals on candle magic, meditation techniques, breath, color, making incense with herbs, working with oils and herbs, and the list goes on.

I spent a lot of money on all of the different topics, becoming frustrated with the fact that none of them were combined in simple techniques to facilitate change in the human body. I wanted *that* book!

While working with various clients in my healing and psychic practice, I found myself recommending many different books to my clients. I rattled off numerous titles of all the books I could think of, secretly wishing I could offer them one healing primer that would guide them through the basic steps of healing the soul, opening up their intuition and guiding them into emotional balance.

I continued to search and research, finding significant benefits from using aroma, herbs, oils, candles, meditation, releasing of emotions, visualization and self-talk to better ones self. It was working for me in my own life, why couldn't it work for others?

This took me into offering classes and teaching the combined techniques to my clients. I thrived on watching the individual changes that occurred, logging it all in my journal, along with the various methods I used to help facilitate those changes and how the students reacted to them. It was exciting and satisfying to see the changes in the people around me and in myself.

I took what I knew further and began researching herbs in particular. Scott Cunningham's *Incense, Oils and Brews* led me into playing with herbs and the different combinations of herbal mixtures. It was fun to create incense out of leaves and flowers. I liked the way it felt and the way my body reacted as I mixed, poured and experimented with the recipes. It was a new adventure each time I worked on creating the recipes he suggested, and then it shifted.

I had worked through all of his recipes and combined techniques. I went back through and took what I had learned, taking it a step further through adding energy and intention to the mixing process. I logged those experiments as well, indicating how my body felt, what happened while creating different mixtures and how it could affect others when burned in class.

A few months after discovering how to make Incense, a series of significant teachers entered my life. I became an in-house Psychic at a store in Colorado, called Metamorphosis. I was suddenly part of a circle of healers who shared their wisdom freely and offered up new ways to heal, move energy in the body, and who, much to my delight, worked with herbs and oils. My indoctrination into the various healing modalities began the day I entered Metamorphosis Bookstore.

I was privileged to be in the midst of some amazing healers; High Priestesses of Hawaiian Magick, Wicca, Reiki Masters, Tarot Readers, Crystal Healers and Light Workers. My lessons became a daily process of being deeply in-tune with my own wounds, releasing them and acknowledging what I needed to work on in my own life. I had the added benefit of listening to various clients who mirrored back to me all the wounds I needed to look at. My entire life was an energetic school of healing, all designed to shift my energy and heal my soul.

For seven years I worked in and around that little shop of miracles, all the while playing with different ways to facilitate healing on a soul level with various energetic tools.

Incense was my favorite. Herbs were like chocolate cake and essential oils were the frosting. They excited me and drove me to experiment more with incense than any other healing tool. My journal expanded as I worked outside the suggestions of Scott Cunningham's books or Wylundt's *Book of Incense*, and all the herbal lore in the wide collection of books I had read.

I practised the techniques of moving energy through the incense and visualizing what the end result would be if I stood over the incense mixtures and meditated. I quickly discovered that not only did my life change rapidly for the better, but doors flung open wide to offer me situations for change that otherwise may not have manifested. This led to the writing of *Scents of the Soul*.

My journal of incense experiments, my own energy explorations and releases, countless hours of counseling clients, and hearing every imaginable crisis situation possible, has helped to make this book happen. Advice, classes, meditations and all the recipes have been offered up to individuals that I have worked with for the past 20 years. Now I am offering them up to you to experiment with, process through, and find your own unique healing tools for your soul.

I must tell you that even though the chapters are based on creating incense mixtures, the intent of this book is to open up your intuition and help you to release old wounds. My goal is to supply you with a variety of healing techniques for yourself and others. The recipes are the catalyst for change. The meditations and ceremonies are the actual healing work. The end result is up to you and how you decide to work with this book. You can create significant changes if you choose to openly and honestly do the work in these pages.

Currently my path has been blessed with teachers from all walks of life who have guided me through meditation techniques, yoga practices; massage and chakra work, healing with crystals and stones, and countless lessons on human suffering. I have been privileged to give psychic-medium readings to clients for the past 28 years and have counseled over 5,000 people in those amazing years of practice.

Spirit has guided me to study with Native American Shamans, Herbalists, Astrologers, Psychics, Reiki Masters and Lightworkers' from around the globe. I have had so many incredible teachers, some famous, most not, who have guided me into the work I do now. I am eternally grateful and blessed to be able to share some of those lessons with you.

My life has shifted from devoting my life to studying herbs to studying to achieve my Phd in Metaphysical Sciences with the University of Metaphysical Sciences in California. I continue to write and offer readings all over the world. I am married to a magnificent man who is my soul twin and best friend for the past five years, and who joins me in the garden on the weekends to tend to the herbs and weed the vegetable garden. I have two lovely grown children, who live in Colorado. I am very proud of them as they are traveling their own paths of self-discovery.

My path continues to morph into teaching, seminars and working continually with my own soul growth. As you work through the pages of this book, *the* book I searched for so long, I wish for you enlightenment and healing, enjoyment and change as you play with the herbs and explore your own individual Scents of the Soul.

Introduction

WELCOME to the world of herbs, incense, energy work and meditation. If you have picked up this book, chances are the subtle energies of the Universe guided you to its pages. In working through the recipes that are offered here, you will be awakening your soul's energy and transforming it to a much higher state of awareness.

You will learn about natural healing, herbs, essential oils, energy and how to make energy move. You will experience techniques designed to assist you in focusing energy while creating results through meditation and intention. You will access the Spirit Realm, Earthly Realm, and the Realm of Self Awareness while mixing and creating yummy herbal recipes to assist you in opening up your energy.

Included in this 'cookbook of energy' are instructions on the use of candle magic, meditation, manifesting prosperity, finding love, and attracting your Guides and Angels. Your life will naturally become enhanced by working with the herbs and allowing the energetic process to flow through your mind, body and soul.

With every exercise I have incorporated into this energetic workbook, you will find hidden parts of your intuitive awareness "waking up" and making themselves known to you. You won't be creating an ordinary incense recipe, more a special way to facilitate energetic shifts and releases in your life. As the title suggests it is about creating herbal incense for body, mind and spirit.

Over the years, I have been fortunate to have had the honor of observing people change their lives by making small differences in their energetic environment. I started this process, in much the same way as this book is written; by following the exercises, doing each meditation and then journaling my own transformations.

The key to being successful while using this book is to practice, practice, and practice some more! Read as much as you can. Create as much energetic healing for yourself as you can. Move your energy. Do the meditations, then be the observer as your life begins to open up to the creation of your own personal miracles.

All the research, herbal information, essential oil mixing, energy work, meditations, chakra clearing, and different aspects of personal healing, are included here. This book is a primer to guide you into your own unique path of transformation and awareness.

You will release old hurts, open your Chakras, meet your Guides and Angels, and awaken the very depths of your Soul. The incense recipes will not only create wonderful scents, but the meditations and energy work will assist you in dissolving situations or patterns that keep you from moving forward in your life.

Each yummy incense recipe is created with crushed dried herbs, essential oils, and Reiki (hands on healing energy,) meditation techniques, candle magic techniques, and Chakra clearing. The flow of the book will take you into your senses opening them up gently and teaching you to deepen into your own unique soul awareness. It is a roadmap to open your Chakras, fine- tune your intuition and introduce you to the various forms of energy work.

I strongly recommend keeping a journal to keep track of your progress while moving through the chapters. A journal of your experiences allows you to go back over your work and see your progress. Create your own unique journal of healing.

Enjoy the experience. Have fun with it all, but most of all allow the healing doors of your life to fly open!

Hints & Tips

- You may use herbal substitutions in this cookbook, but be sure they co-ordinate with the properties of the herb you are replacing.

- Each herb and oil is accompanied by its uses and energy. The recipes are designed to roughly create about a cup of loose, powdered incense.

- Enjoy yourself while you play with the recipes. Experiment with the different herbal combinations when the mood hits you to try something else. Allow the energy work to take you on a wondrous journey of self-discovery and leave you with a new, fresh reality full of healing and joy.

I wish you many blessings and a playful journey as you begin mixing your way into the scents of your soul.

CHAPTER 1

Getting Started

Guidelines

BEFORE starting your energy adventure, there are a few tips I would like to share with you. Always trust your "gut" reactions to the exercises and recipes in this book. Your instincts will *always* be right and your head will *always* try to talk you out of those instinctual reactions.

As you create the incense recipes, try to keep positive energy flowing through your thoughts and actions. All energy work should be practised from a respectful, loving intention. Negative energy will disrupt the outcome of the incense and the personal energy work you will be doing while creating the recipes.

You will process emotionally. You may experience uncomfortable feelings coming up from time to time as you are preparing the incense recipes. Go with it! It's all part of letting the energy shift. Let the feelings happen without stopping them. Do not be fearful of crying, laughing, and becoming angry. Allowing feelings to come up and be noticed is an important part of moving forward in life and becoming emotionally healthy. Give yourself plenty of time to react if you need to do so. Honor what you are feeling.

1. **A journal.** Keep a journal of your thoughts, feelings and your own recipe ideas as you work with this book. You will find your journal to be a priceless investment in yourself.

2. **Have no set expectations.** Expectations limit what you can create. They shut off how you manifest your intentions. The Universe shifts energy in many surprising ways. The way you picture change may be different than how it may come about. Go with the flow! No expectations create pure thought forms.

3. **Have fun with the meditations and recipes!** Making change happen in your life is an exciting goal. Play with it!

   Know that the recipes and meditations are designed for the highest good of all involved. They are not designed to harm, hurt or manipulate anyone!

4. **Drink lots of water.** As you do this work, remember to take good care of your body. Moving energy burns *your* energy. Dehydration is a common side effect of doing healing exercises, so drink plenty of water or a healthy sports drink to replenish what you burn.

   Energy work will enable you to make changes in your life. Sometimes these changes will be swift, very noticeable and at times uncomfortable. Other changes will occur in a more subtle way. Pay attention to those changes no matter how minute they may be. Little ripples of change can bring about big results in the end. You will find yourself experiencing healing and a heightened sensitivity to your own feelings and perhaps to the feelings of those around you. Be aware of those sensitivities and honor them.

Tools And Supplies

As you work with this book, you will need certain tools, which are easily obtainable and relatively inexpensive. Below are the materials and tools that you will use while making the recipes:

- 2 bowls – one for mixing – one for experimenting.
- Spoon, mortar and pestle for mixing, crushing and preparing the herbs. A blender is acceptable for crushing and stirring to achieve very fine powders. (*Note, blenders are messy but effective for fine grinding. Coffee grinders work well also.*)
- Two or three eyedroppers for oils.
- Baggies or bottles to store incense, oils and herbs.
- Charcoal briquettes for burning incense. Name brands are Three Kings and Swift Lite.
- A shallow incense burner, either cauldron shaped or round brass burners. (*Put sand or cat litter in it to fill the depth. Charcoal cannot "breathe" in a deep burner*).

- Labels for bagged incense and herbs. Labels from any local cooking shop or garden shop. File labels work great too!
- Journal and pen.
- Sage wand for energetically cleansing tools. (*White Sage is my personal favorite. It is now an endangered species of Herb and rather hard to get. Sweet Grass or Frankincense Resin works fine as a substitute for White Sage*).

Before creating powdered Incense you will "charge" the tools you are going to be using. Charging simply means clearing any negative energy from an object or person and raising the object or person's energy levels. Sage wands, Frankincense Resin, and Sweet Grass are all used for this very purpose.

You can find Sweet Grass, Frankincense and Sage at most metaphysical stores and sometimes at health food stores. You can also order any of the above listed herbs or resins on the Internet. Resources are listed at the back of this book.

To cleanse the tools you will be using, begin by lighting the end of the Sage wand. When using a Sage wand, let the ends burn brightly. Gently blow the smoke towards your tools, letting the smoke wrap around them. Visualize any negative vibrations releasing with the smoke.

If you are using charcoal for resin, light the edge of the charcoal. When the charcoal is hot, gray or red around the edges add a pinch of the resin. Run the tools above the resin smoke, visualizing any negativity releasing from them.

When you have finished cleansing all of the tools, let the wand's smoke clear away the negative energy that may be in your workspace. Walk clockwise around the room you are working in. Visualize the smoke clearing the room and raising the positive vibrations to prepare for the energy work you will be doing in the following chapters.

Lightly move the wand around yourself. Move the negativity that may be on or around you away from your body. This will cleanse your Aura. You will find a peaceful, almost floating feeling occurring. Visualize your personal energy levels rising. Release the worries of the day and dissolve away the negativity with the smoke.

When you have finished the clearing, place the Sage wand in a bowl of sand to put out the fire or rub the end of the wand against the bowl, releasing the burned ends. If you are using charcoal, place the burner outside, letting the remaining resin burn away.

Now you will fill the tools back up with energy. Place them in the sun or in moonlight. Solar or Lunar energy is a fantastic way to amp up the energy already in the tools you will be using! If you choose to charge your tools in the moon or the sunlight, please know that all things fiery, like a knife, an incense burner or anything that is used in a fiery way should go in the sunlight.

Watery tools, such as a blender, oil bottles, chalices, bottles, bowl, mortar and pestle or spoon, should be placed in the moonlight.

Log how you felt while doing this exercise. Be explicit in logging your feelings, body reactions, and any pain you might have felt in your body.

CHAPTER 2

Ingredients –
Herbs & Essential Oils

HERBS are perhaps the most versatile tools you can use. Herbs containing the very best energy are those grown, nourished, harvested and dried by you.

Many people are urban herbalists, unable to grow and maintain large amounts of herbs to use for magical, healing blends. We are limited by time and space. For time purposes and ease in working with this book, all the recipes here were created with dried herbs. You can purchase dried Herbs through wholesale companies or at local metaphysical/health food stores, the Internet or from the list of reputable suppliers in the back of this book.

Follow these simple guidelines when purchasing dried herbs. This will ensure you get the best products for the incense preparation.

- Check for freshness. Most herbs have strong odors. If there is little or no odor, chances are the herbs are not fresh.
- Look for mold on the dried flowers, the leaves and stems. It will appear as white fuzzy stuff or black dots on the leaves. Inspect the herbs for insects that may have not been cleaned out of the foliage at the drying stage.
- Make sure the herbs you are buying at the grocery or health food store are being stored in air tight, filtered containers. Light and heat can destroy the properties of herbs. Light can destroy the aromatics of an herb, so buy with caution to ensure the freshest quality plants.
- Shop around to find the best herbs with competitive prices. If you look hard, sometimes you can find that little unknown metaphysical store that carries a delightful selection of herbs or a health food store that carries fresh herbs you can hang and dry yourself.

When you have purchased the herbs you want to work with and are ready to store them, put them into airtight containers such as amber or blue bottles. Brown paper bags with the zip locked bags, safely tucked inside away from sunlight or air, work well too.

Buy labels that are big enough to write the names and properties of each herb on, for easy reference. As time goes by, you will of course develop your own unique system to label, package and store your herbs and oils.

Essential Oils

An essential oil is extracted from different species of flowers, grasses, fruits, leaves, bark, resins, roots and trees. Do not be fooled by "perfume" or "fragrance" oils. These are usually man-made, containing little to no actual oil, but a heavy amount of alcohol or filler oil that is not pure essential extract. Look on the back labels to inspect for alcohol or additives. Most Perfume oils will say they are perfume mixes. Perfumes burn quite heavy and can be very toxic depending on their base mixture.

Aromatherapy

A method by which the use of certain essential oils are either combined or used alone to promote healing and well being by applying the oils directly to the body or by inhalation.

Synergy

Combining two or more oils will bring about a more powerful effect. Mixing oils together creates a chemical compound that is different from the single oil. An increased potency can be achieved through a synergistic blend without increasing the dosage.

Carrier or Base Oil

Oils that have no aroma are used to dilute the highly concentrated essential oils. They are used for massage oils; roll on scents, hand creams and bath salts. Oils are made from vegetables, nuts or seeds, many of which have therapeutic properties of their own.

Essential and Base Oils are available at most health food and metaphysical stores. I have listed some excellent wholesale suppliers in the back of this book.

CHAPTER 3

Love Incense Recipe – Meditation & Ceremony

THE FOLLOWING incense recipes are created in loose powder form as opposed to cone or stick incense. I prefer loose incense because of the energy created in the mixing process. Powdered herbs, combined with oils, bring about powerful, energetic change. I have included the energies each herb resonates to, for quick reference.

If you choose to substitute any herbs, log them in a journal for future reference. Keeping an exact log of what you substituted, what scents you liked, and how you felt during the mixing or burning will prove invaluable to you. You may also choose to recreate the mixtures in the future, either for selling to others, for your own personal use or for gifts.

HERBS YOU WILL NEED:

- 2 Tbls. Allspice – Increases positive vibrations in the body, creates feelings of love.
- ½ cup Patchouli – Stimulates the heart to share unconditional love.
- 2 tsps. Vervain – Opens the heart to accept love, creates peace and harmony, and increases feelings of sexuality.
- 1 Tonka Bean ground – Connects the body to the earth, inspires feelings of love, peace, and prosperity.
- 1 ½ handfuls of Rose Flowers (red or pink) – Inspiration, transformation and love.
- 2 tsps. Benzoin Gum Powder to bind the mixture and raise vibrations in the herbs.
- ½ cup pine sawdust (optional)

ESSENTIAL OILS YOU WILL NEED:

- 5 drops Rose oil – Opens the heart to unconditional love.
- 3 drops Pennyroyal oil – Creates peaceful, loving feelings.
- 5 to 10 drops Red or Pink food coloring.

Before adding the herbs to the mixing bowl notice how the herbs feel in your hand. Feel the texture, the shape and the sensations you have while holding the herbs. Pay attention to how your body feels as you connect to the herbs. Close your eyes and breathe. Pay attention to the places in your body that respond positively or negatively to the herbs. Record these feelings in your journal.

Now add all the dry ingredients to the mixing bowl. Begin crushing the herbs slowly and deliberately with the pestle and mortar. As you crunch the herbs, visualize love emitting from the flowers, spices and beans. Feel the way your body reacts to the sensations of mixing this deliciously, aromatic love mixture.

The herbs may be crushed as finely as you like or you may leave some of the petals whole in the mixture. Grind the sawdust in the blender until it is ground very fine. *Pine shavings are often used as a binder and filler for incense. If you prefer to have this mixture without the sawdust, you will have the same result energetically.*

Add the food coloring to the sawdust. *Red and pink resonate to the energy of Love.* Simply put a few drops of food coloring into the cup of shavings and stir them around, covering the shavings. You can mix them up in a zip lock baggie as well, shaking them up and down, and distributing the color through the dust.

When you have completed crushing the herbs and have added the shavings, add the wet ingredients. If you happen to add a drop or two more of the essential oils do not worry, it all mixes in and will simply make the incense a little bit stronger than the recipe calls for. You may like it that way! *Be sure to stir after each essential oil has been added to ensure that the mixture is completely blended.*

Add the Benzoin Gum powder. Benzoin is designed to bond the herbs further, raising the vibrations of the mixture and prolonging the burning time of the incense. Now the Incense is ready to test for scent. Light a charcoal briquette. The briquette will sparkle and crackle with the edges turning bright orange. Drop the briquette in the burner being careful not to burn your fingers. When the charcoal is gray around the edges begin adding the Love Incense.

Place a pinch of the freshly made Love Incense on the charcoal. Pull the smoke towards you with your hands, gently smelling the aroma of the incense. *DO NOT put your face over the smoke! It tends to irritate sinuses if it is inhaled directly.*

How does the smell make your body feel? Does your body hurt anywhere? Do you like the smell? Is the smell too weak? Feel free to add more essential oils to create the intensity you like.

Check the mixture every few drops to make sure you do not "over scent" the recipe. Smell the incense again. If you are satisfied with the fragrance, and it makes you feel good, then it is time to move on to the energy work.

Energizing or programming the incense is perhaps the single most important step in creating a mixture that will assist in changing your life.

Place the incense in another clean bowl. Hold your hands palms down, over the bowl of Love Incense. Take a few deep breaths in through your nose. Send the breath down through your body. Take another deep breath. Visualize white light, higher power, and spirit coming into your body through your nose.

Feel that wonderful white light clearing any negative energy. Release your breath. Let all the tightness or negativity in your body blow out through your mouth. Take one more deep breath. Visualize pink light coming in through your nose. Expand the pink light up and down your body.

If you have trouble visualizing the color pink or white, think about the word Pink or the word White. See the words as if they are posted up on a giant movie screen. Your body will resonate to the visualization and allow the energy to move through you.

Pink light represents unconditional love. Breathing it opens up the heart area, allowing us to give and receive love. As you take the next breath of Pink Light in through your nose, send that energy down through your body and into your hands.

Direct the radiant pink, unconditional love energy into the bowl of incense. Fill it with that same unconditional love you are now experiencing.

You may feel hot or cold as you do this procedure. Let it happen! You are simply moving energy. If you feel sadness or elation, don't fight those feelings or question them. Let them come up and move out of you. Energy movement is designed to make you process out your deepest emotions.

When you feel like you have sent enough pink light into the incense, shake your hands out at your side, visualizing the energy falling off and away from your hands. This is called *grounding out the energy.*

Make sure you do this every time you do the energy work. It will help balance and connect you with the 'here and now'. If you feel too spacey or off- balance, light-headed or disoriented, touch the ground with the palms of your hands. Allow Mother Earth's strong, grounding energy to absorb into your hands.

Now that you are fully "back" from your experience, label your newly created Love Incense and add the properties of the herbs on the label. Log in your journal all the feelings that came up for you while you made this mixture.

Add any changes or substitutions as well. When you are finished with labeling and journaling, we will move onto a simple love meditation and ceremony.

Love Meditation And Ceremony

YOU WILL NEED:

- Two pink taper candles.
- Two candle holders.
- Charcoal.
- Love incense.
- An incense burner that will hold charcoal.
- Matches or a lighter.
- Rose petals fresh or dried
- A metal pan.

Sprinkle fresh rose petals around the candleholders. They are pretty and smell wonderful! The roses will inspire you to concentrate on love vibrations before you begin the energy work.

Light the charcoal and place it in the incense burner. Put the pink candles in the candleholders. Sprinkle the rose petals around the candleholders. As you do this, think about what kind of love energy you would like to create for yourself.

This can be anything, from bringing in an unconditional relationship to new friends. Concentrate on the love you want to create and then write it down on a piece of paper. *Be explicit.*

But if you want to create a relationship and you have a specific person in mind, *do not mention that person's name! It is manipulative to change another person's energy without permission.* You may however, think about the qualities of that specific person and what it is that attracts you to them and write those qualities down.

When you have completed writing down the kind of energy you would like to create set aside the paper. You will come back to it after the candles have been placed in their appropriate spots.

Place the pink candles across from each other, leaving a gap between them. Light the first pink candle, the one on your left, while thinking about sending unconditional love out to the Universe and to all the people you know.

Place a pinch of Love Incense on the charcoal. Smell the aroma, paying attention to the way your body is opening up to the electric energy of love. *Let it happen, don't fight it.*

If you feel any resistance or nothing at all, breathe in or think about pink light. Send the pink light to the areas in your body that feel blocked or in pain as you do this exercise. Blow out deep breaths through your mouth. Release any tension or pain you may be experiencing.

Go back to the piece of paper you wrote your wishes on. Read the things you have written down out loud. Really *"feel"* what you have written, thinking again of the unconditional love you want to create.

If you are doing this to create an unconditional, loving relationship, visualize that energy. If you want to attract friends, improve family relationships, or bring new people into your life, feel it, see it, know it throughout your heart and body!

Put another pinch of Love Incense on the charcoal. Pay close attention to your body. How is it reacting to the energy work you are doing? What sensations are coming up and out of your body? Does your body hurt in any specific places? Be sure and log these feelings in your journal.

If your chest is tight or you are experiencing pain behind your shoulder blades, you have old love issues to release. If you have pain in your hips, this represents not feeling supported by a loved one. If your neck hurts, ask yourself what loved one is being a pain in the neck?

Let the pink candles burn for about an hour. Check on them off and on during the time they are burning. Each time you reconnect with the candles visualize incredible love energy spreading all around you.

Let the candles burn almost to the end of the taper. When they are close to burning all the way out, burn the piece of paper with your wishes on it. Send those precious wishes out to the Universe. Place the ashes of paper in a metal pan. When the ashes have cooled, take them outside and release them to the wind, sending your intentions out to spirit.

You may do this meditation for the next three days if you have the time to devote to it. For the next two days every time you relight the pink candles, do the visualization work and move the candles a little bit closer together. This symbolizes unconditional love coming in to you as well as going out to the Universe.

By the end of the third day the candles should be burned to the end of the taper. You will see the love energy changing all around you.

Pay attention to all the love that will shower down around you after you do this exercise. Log all your reactions, including feelings of sadness and joy. Sometimes love is not always happy.

It can bring up deep childhood emotions of neglect, sadness or abandonment. Honor whatever feelings you experience and let them filter through you, cleansing any negativity that may accompany the feelings you are processing from this meditation.

Never blow out candles while using them for candle work. It disperses the energy you are trying to create. Snuff them with a candlesnuffer or with your fingers. If you are relighting candles used for a continued meditation or energy work, thank the candles. Ask them to hold the energy you have placed in them until they are lit again.

CHAPTER 4

Prosperity Incense – Recipe & Visualization

HERBS YOU WILL NEED:

- 2 tsps. Allspice – Connects the body to earthiness and love.
- ¼ cup Basil – Creates wealth and harmony.
- ¼ cup Calamus – Opens the emotions, attracts wealth and harmony.
- 2 roots ground fresh or ¼ cup pre-ground Galangal - Manifests money, and clears negativity.
- ½ cup Peppermint - Magnetizes energies of wealth and prosperity.
- ¼ cup Pine Sawdust (Optional)

ESSENTIAL OILS YOU WILL NEED:

- 18 drops Peppermint Oil – Attracts money, stimulates positive energy.
- 10 drops Green Food Coloring (optional)

Mix the dry ingredients together in a mixing bowl. Pay attention to the way the herbs feel, smell and affect your body as you mix them together. After mixing the dry ingredients, including the ground sawdust, add the oils. *Stir after each addition of oil to control how much scent you are adding.* If at anytime you feel the scent is too strong and you have not added all the oils in the recipe, listen to your senses. Add what feels and smells right to you.

Burn a sample of the Prosperity Incense, adjusting the oils as you see fit. Add a pinch of the Basil and Peppermint loosely after mixing. You will find that it smells really wonderful.

If you add too much loose Basil, it will burn with a pungent odor. Add a tiny amount to increase the attraction of money to your mixture.

Finish it off with a few drops of food coloring, adding it slowly to get the desired color you like. You may blend the coloring in the blender or shake it up in a zip lock bag (the blender is easier). Adjust the color by adding as many or as few drops of green food coloring as you like. *The color green attracts the energy of money, new beginnings, and prosperity.*

Test the Prosperity Incense again on the charcoal, making sure the smell is to your liking. If it does not smell "minty" enough add a few more drops of Peppermint oil. Stir, test it and bag it up. Make sure you label the incense and log any substitutions in your journal.

Charging Incense

Transfer the Prosperity Incense into a clean bowl. Place your hands over the incense, palms down. Take a few deep cleansing breaths in through your nose.

Blow out through your mouth allowing any blocks in your body to release as you exhale. Inhale through your nose again visualizing and feeling green light. Send the green light all the way through your body and release your breath through your mouth. (Pause Here).

Again inhale the green light through your nose, this time sending the green light down through your hands and into the Prosperity Incense. Green light represents new beginnings, an open heart, earth, abundance, and prosperity.

As you send the green light into the bowl of incense, think about money coming to you from the Universe. Visualize prosperity and abundance being created in every aspect of your life.

In your mind imagine money, abundance and joy all around you. Let your mind and body show you what kind of money you can attract. What you think about will result in manifesting. Simply focusing on that thought can create a wealth of new beginnings and attract those things which have seemed somewhat out of reach previously. Incense, energy movement, and intense visualizing assist in the manifestation process you are currently practising as you charge the incense recipe.

Let your imagination run wild, visualizing winning the lottery even! Perhaps you need to make a career move that would be financially better for you. Imagine buying that perfect dream house and having the funds to do that. Let your senses show you what desires you have in your heart that need to be manifested right now. Breathe through it and into it, letting the green light of Prosperity inspire your ability to create what you need and want in your life.

When you feel like you have thoroughly charged the incense and have come to the end of your imaginative exploration of your abundant desires, package the

Prosperity Incense, label it, and remember to log any substitutions you may have used. Be sure to write down the feelings you experienced or insights you found while making this recipe.

Pay attention to the places in your body that feel good. Perhaps you feel blocked or are experiencing pain as you prepared the incense. Notice where that pain is occurring for this is where you hold your various money issues.

Pain in the body that occurs while doing energy work acts as a barometer to clue you into any physical/energetic blocks you may have. Those blockages are created through lessons learned throughout your lifetime. In doing prosperity work, breathing Green Light into those places that might have energy blocks, helps to heal those issues.

For instance, if your back is hurting right now, you do not feel supported by others in your work or financially. If you feel pain in your shoulders you feel overwhelmed with responsibilities. If your lower back is hurting, you are in survival mode. If your neck is aching, you have someone around you that is being a pain in the neck where money is concerned.

Pay attention to these reactions! Your body will always give you clues to what's really going on.

When you have clarified what hurts or is blocked, do the breath work to relieve that pain. When you release the blockages in your energetic/physical body prosperity is once again allowed to flow through you and around you.

Log your feelings and any work or "Ah-Ha" moments you may have experienced in making the Prosperity Incense. We will move on to the Prosperity visualization.

Prosperity Visualization And Ceremony

YOU WILL NEED:

- 1 green taper candle
- 1 candle holder
- A charcoal briquette
- An incense holder
- Peppermint oil
- A pen or sharp dinner knife.

Light the charcoal briquette and place it in the incense holder. Think about the kind of prosperity you would like to create in your life. As you do this, hold the green taper candle between your palms. Visualize the kind of money or belongings you would like to see come to you. (This also works for creating a new job or moving forward in the job you have).

Thank the Universe, God, and Spirit, whatever you believe in, for the abundance you already have. Gratitude is the first step to really acknowledging your own abundance. Being grateful for the gifts Spirit has already bestowed upon you reinforces abundance and prepares you to create more.

Write what it is you would like to give thanks for on the candle. Write from the top of the candle to the bottom of the candle. (You can write this with a knife or a pen). Now write what you would like to create on your candle. *Be very specific! You do not have to be able to read what you wrote because you are simply placing the energy of your intentions on the candle.*

It is perfectly acceptable to write over what you have written. You are charging this candle with your positive, non-manipulative intentions. The Universe doesn't really grade on penmanship or spelling, only manifestation.

Be specific in your needs. Do you want a new job? Do you need a new car? Perhaps you want a new home. Maybe paying off your bills is your focus. Write it down and be very specific! *The more specific you are the faster change will occur.*

When you have finished writing your desires, explicitly, on the candle, pour a small amount of Peppermint Oil onto your left palm. Run the candle through the oil, from the middle to the base of the candle, swiping the candle through the oil.

Visualize all negativity releasing from the candle as you do this. Turn the candle around and run it from the middle of the candle to the top of the candle. Imagine all your wishes and intentions going to the Universe with every stroke of the candle. This is called "dressing" the candle.

The aroma of the oil, the energy from your palm, and the positive intentions you wrote on the candle all "charge" the candle with specific energy so the Universe can bring you what you ask for.

Place the candle in the candleholder and light it. Direct your focus to the specific intentions you want to create in your life. While the candle burns to the end of the taper, be sure to connect with it periodically. Staying connected to the energy while the candle burns magnifies the energy you are putting out to the Universe, accelerating the manifestation process.

In doing this particular visualization, you may be as creative and fantasy-based as you like. I have been a stunned witness to clients winning the lottery after doing this visualization. It may have been only a small amount, but they did win. Sometimes the things they wished for came in unusual ways, such as the lady who wished for a brand new car so she could get rid of her old junky one.

This particular woman, left my class, got in her car and got hit by another car on her way home. She was not hurt, but her junky car was totaled. Her insurance paid for her brand new car and relieved her of the one she was having so much trouble with.

It is so important to be extremely positive and specific in what you want when doing this exercise. If the Universe is told exactly what your wants and desires are, you will be given those specific things easily and gently.

The Universe loves to answer your call but sometimes it occurs in unusual, funny ways. That doesn't mean that because you did this particular exercise, Aunt Glenda is suddenly going to croak and leave you a bunch of hidden money. No, it means that a loved one might just hand you money or property you were not expecting.

When you are finished with the visualization, log your reactions to the Prosperity Ceremony. Write down how your body felt while burning the prosperity incense and doing the candle work.

Watch for various surprises of abundance and prosperity as the Universe responds to your intentions. Log these in your journal as well. Drink plenty of fluids and replenish your energy. You did a great job!

CHAPTER 5

Faerie and Elf Incense – Recipe & Meditation

The following recipes are dedicated to my 'Elvin brother', Griff.

FAERIE INCENSE – HERBS YOU WILL NEED:

- ½ cup Sandalwood chips – Enhances intuition, and calls in spirits.
- 4 tbl. Hawthorne Berries – Raises feelings of passion, attracts fairies, and animals.
- 4 Tbls. Pippesewa – Inspires romance, attracts spirits, and happiness.
- ¾ cup Rose petals (any color) – Creates feelings of love, inspiration, beauty, magic, and an open heart.
- 1Tbl. Benzoin Gum – Binder.
- A pinch or two of ground Amber Resin - Unconditional love, earth and faeries.
- 1 cup Saw Dust (Optional)

ESSENTIAL OILS YOU WILL NEED:

- 5 drops Cedarwood Oil. – Attracts faeries, clears negativity.
- 5 drops Pennyroyal Oil – Calls faeries, opens the heart center.
- 1 drop Amber oil – Balances the body and enhances wisdom from past lives.

Turn on some happy, lighthearted music and invite the Faerie Realm into your home. Open a window and strap on your faerie wings. Prepare to have some wispy, airy, energetic fun!

Mix the herbs, *except* for the Hawthorne Berries and Amber Resin. These you will add later.

You may want to grind this particular mixture in a blender for finer incense especially if you are adding bark.

Add the Benzoin Gum to bind the herbs. Remove the mixture from the blender. Add the oils. With every drop of oil, visualize inviting Faeries to come into your home. Imagine them flying around your ceiling. See them flitting around your head, filling your heart with joy. Pay attention to how you feel as you mix the herbs with the oils. Log this in your journal.

Add the Amber. Add the Hawthorne Berries. *DO NOT grind them up!* Add a handful of the dried flower petals after you have everything mixed. Do not grind the flower petals. They look pretty and smell nice as the incense burns.

Make sure you pick nice smelling flower petals like Violets and Roses. Be aware of tinkling noises you may hear or birds singing in your yard. You may be treated to light fragile sounds, gliding around your head. The Fey Folk are letting you know they are with you helping to mix the incense.

Test the incense blend on a hot charcoal. If you need to add more oils do so. Visualize the Faerie Realm coming in with every drop. This incense is created to smell woodsy and flowery at the same time, so add oils until you feel and smell the earthy quality coming through. Log what you used in your journal and be sure to log any substitutions or experiences you had while playing with the Faerie Folk.

ELVIN INCENSE – HERBS YOU WILL NEED:

- ½ cup Tree Bark (optional) – Creates feelings of power, earthiness, and woodlands.
- Aspen, Ash or Pine barks are nice. Ash traditionally attracts elves and faeries.
- ½ cup Dried Flower Petals (optional) – Love, softness, and earth.
- ¼ cup Fallen Leaves (optional) – Strength, earth, and woodlands.
- ½ cup Rowan Berries Whole – Attracts elves, protection, and luck.
- ½ cup dried Violet Flowers – Inspires romance, beauty, and raises intuition to contact other Realms.
- ½ cup Angelica – Opens the heart to love and dreams.
- ½ cup White Willow Bark – Cleanses the emotions, attracts elves, and

heightens intuition.
- ½ cup Elecampane – Heightens communication with the earth, animals, and elves.
- 2 Tbls. Benzoin Gum – Binder.

ESSENTIAL OILS YOU WILL NEED:

- 7 drops Thyme oil – Attracts elves and magical encounters.
- 4 drops Tea Tree oil – Purifies energy and attracts elves.
- 4 drops Pine Oil – Manifests money and protection.
- 10 drops Green Food Coloring (Optional)

Blend the dried herbs together *except* for the Rowan Berries. The berries will be added last and will not be ground. Add the Benzoin Gum to bind the herbs. Remove the mixture from the blender and place in a mixing bowl. Add the Rowan Berries. Begin to add the Thyme oil drop by drop.

Visualize the Elvin Realm, Leprechauns, Brownies, and all the "Wee Folk" coming to you with every drop of oil. Imagine these earthy creatures bringing you gifts, such as special stones, crystals, leaves and flowers.

You may feel many body sensations as you visualize the gifts. Pay attention to them and do not be alarmed. The Elvin Folk are simply letting you know they are all around you.

Add the Tea Tree Oil and Pine Oil. Mix the oils together with the herbs. Continue inviting the Elvin Realm into your home as you work. Log how you are feeling while you mix the herbs and oils. Do you want to laugh and sing? Do you feel like going outside and playing? Are you feeling intensely earthy and a bit mischievous? Maybe you feel nothing at all. That is perfectly alright. Those energies are coming in whether you feel them or not. Be sure to log all of your reactions.

Now, light the charcoal briquette and sample your Elvin creation. Pay attention to your body and the reactions that occur while you feel and smell the scent. If you need to add more oils to get the scent to where you like it, do so now.

The Pine oil absorbs quickly into the herbs, so you may want to experiment with that one first.

When you feel finished with the mixing process, package the Elf Incense remembering to log the herbal substitutions you may have used for the barks and flowers.

FAERIE AND ELF MEDITATION – ITEMS YOU WILL NEED:

- Music (optional). Celtic music tends to resonate well with the "Wee Folk." "Light" meditation music is suggested, like Loreena McKennitt CDs or Landscapes Music Line available at retail centers like Wal-mart or Target Stores.
- 1 Green candle
- 1 Candle holder
- Pine oil
- Charcoal
- An incense burner
- Faerie and Elf Incense

Before you begin this meditation, you may want to read it into a tape recorder. You can then relax and get into the energy much easier if you are not struggling with reading and letting go all at the same time.

Music is a wonderful tool for meditating. Feeling the music resonating through your body will help to create healing and assist you in focusing on the experience.

To begin the meditative process, start whatever music you have chosen. Place a few drops of Pine oil in your left palm. Run the green candle from the middle of your palm, downward through the oil. Think about releasing any negative energy that may have been on the candle before it came to you. Turn the candle around and repeat the process from the middle upwards going towards the wick. This is called *"dressing the candle."* Allow airy fairy energy to come into your candle as you think about inviting the Elvin and Fairy Folk into your quiet place.

Place the candle in the candleholder after you have finished dressing the candle. Light the charcoal. Place it in the burner as it gets very hot and gray around the edges. Place a small amount of either Elf or Fairy incense on the charcoal.

Sit in a comfortable position on the floor or on a cushion, whatever makes you feel comfortable. Take a few deep breaths in through your nose and out through your mouth to relax your body. Pay attention to any aches or pains that may be in your body.

Send cleansing breath into the painful areas, filling your lungs completely and then releasing the pain through your breath. With your next breath, breathe in white light through your nose and send it down through your entire body. Release any anxiety or stress you feel through your mouth.

*This is called "circular breathing." It is an ancient form of breathing
designed to fill your body with oxygen and cleanse your lungs. This will
help you to relax and prepare for meditation.*

Begin to visualize yourself in a forest surrounded with lush, beautiful trees. There
are trees of all kinds stretching around you. They are touching the sky with their
long limbs and graceful leaves. Begin walking through the trees. Listen to the
sounds of the forest and all the creatures in it.

You become aware of a dirt path that is leading you into a serene meadow full
of flowers and butterflies. As you approach the meadow, a tiny voice calls to you.
"Come into the meadow, come into the meadow. Come join the Wee Folk as we
dance and play. Come join with us."

You are comfortable with the voice and the invitation, Begin to walk, skip or
dance into the meadow. You become aware of tiny figures in the tall grass. Small,
delightful Faeries are peeking through the slender shoots of green. They look at
you from around the flower stems. You marvel at the sights and sounds of the lush
meadow, while a small Faerie lands on your left shoulder. She laughs lightly in your
ear, tickling your neck with her whispers. She invites you to walk further into the
meadow with her.

You become aware of miniature, gossamer-winged Faeries dancing and giggling
above your head. They invite you to join them. They want to frolic and play with
you. You feel their joy and a sense of contentment fills you. *(Pause.)*

Music begins to play and your body begins to sway to the sounds. The dancing
begins and you join them. You feel so free and light. Your own laughter mingles with
the vibrancy of the Fairies. Allow your body to move. Become light as a feather, releasing any worries or stress as you dance. *(Pause.)*

A single, tiny voice rises above the music and dancing. You notice a beautiful
Faerie perched on your shoulder. She has a message for you. Pay attention to the
message as her voice comes into your thoughts. *(Pause.)*

You resume the dance, moving and circling with the Fey releasing your worries,
letting go of your fears, filling your Soul up with childlike joy. Feel the cleansing
energy of the dance. Let your body go.

When you feel like you have danced enough, sit comfortably in the meadow.
Become aware of your breathing. The Faeries are still dancing as you rest. From the
edge of the Faerie Ring you notice Elvin Folk joining the dance. They laugh and
sing together, raising up energy and sharing the magic of their presence with you.
Feel the energy caressing your body and lifting your mood to pure, joyful serenity.
(Pause.)

You feel your entire body relaxing completely. Take a deep cleansing breath and then focus on the patterns or habits that keep you from being happy. Become aware of what blocks you energetically from being open and childlike.

Think of the blockages you have created for yourself to keep you stuck in negative, blocked energy. Is it your job that has you stuck? Are there people, family members or a relationship that is keeping you from being joyful? Have you stopped yourself from feeling the wonders, becoming aware of your own unique childlike energies?

Clarify the source of these blockages. Take another deep, cleansing breath, blowing out any uncomfortable sensations through your mouth. Now ask yourself these questions:

Do you feel safe? Do you feel loved? Do you feel loveable? Do you feel like you must always be an adult and never a child? *(Pause.)*

Take a deep breath and look at what you need to release in your life to find your childlike happiness. Breathe in deeply, filling yourself with the energy of playfulness. Let the energies of the Faeries and Elves remind you of the wonders of childhood. Now release your breath through the mouth, blowing out any blockages you may be feeling. Feel the tired, worn-out parts of you releasing and flying off to the sky.

Your body is getting lighter. You are standing up in the meadow among the Faeries and Elves. Your body is becoming so much lighter and free as you sway and giggle, letting your feet move you through the meadow.

Release your worries of being an adult and embrace the childlike feeling of dancing with the magic of the Faerie Realm. Dance your way to the edge of the forest where you began this journey. *(Pause.)*

Thank your Faerie and Elvin Guides knowing that they will be with you at all times. You are on the path you started from with the Wee Folk by your side. They wave goodbye as you very slowly travel back up the path to the present time and place. Your body is rejuvenated, full of life and wonder as you become aware of the room you are sitting in, the noises in the room, the sound of your breathing and the beating of your heart. *(Pause.)*

Wiggle your fingers and toes, feeling the sensation of movement in your muscles and body, then place your hands on the floor to ground yourself. When you are ready, open your eyes and let your body stretch. Come back fully to the here and now.

When you feel like you are fully "back" from the meditation, go outside and hug a tree. Feel the earth beneath your feet. Listen to the sounds of the birds, the chirping of bugs and all of Mother Earth's sensational noises and vibrations.

You are keenly aware of everything right now and very much in tune with the

Earth's energy. Acknowledge the beautiful energies of the Faeries and Elves that are tucked away in your own backyard by offering them a small plate of cookies or fruit. When you have completed this meditation, log your experiences in your journal and know that the Realm of Faeries and Elves will always be there to dance with you.

CHAPTER 6

Spirit Calling Incense

NOW that you are aware of what energy is and how to work with it, I would like to introduce you to a higher level of awareness. Spirit Calling Incense allows you to feel spirits. It opens up the energy between our world and their world.

Spirit Calling Incense facilitates the direct communication with those that have crossed to the other side.

The Realm of Spirits is always very close to us. In our daily lives, we forget to acknowledge their presence. We are so busy we ignore the subtle signs of our loved ones trying to get our attention or make contact with us. We completely miss their signs and signals.

If you have never attempted to contact Spirits or have a fear of doing this recipe, the guidelines below will protect you and your energy. The following simple steps are designed to teach you how to listen or be aware of the signs, scents and energies that come through from your Guides, Angels and those that have passed.

The Spirit world is really very gentle when asked to interact with the living. Contacting them simply takes practice, an open mind and a little bit of Spirit Calling Incense to help focus the energy to access their realm.

Spirit Calling Incense will shift your energy dramatically before you ever begin burning it. The herbs suggested for use are very good at raising vibrations whether you actually burn it or not. For this reason, I would like you to take some precautionary steps before you begin mixing.

Please take a few deep breaths. Inhale through your nose and out through your mouth. Release any blocks you may be feeling in your body as you breathe. Relax your neck and shoulders. Let all the stress and worries of the day dissolve into the floor.

Now take a deep breath of white light in through your nose and fill your lungs to the top of your chest. Send the white light down through you body and our through your toes. Allow the radiant white light of healing to circle up around you like a big sleeping bag of comfort and warmth.

Feel yourself completely surrounded in pure white light. Now visualize droplets of bright, shining golden light falling around your head and shoulders. This creates a strong golden bubble of protection.

If you would like to create more sacred space in your home for creating this incense and doing the Spirit Calling meditation, there are various methods you can use before beginning the mixing process.

Sage is an excellent space cleanser, meaning it clears out negative energy that might be around you and removes any unwanted, blocked or negative energy from your personal energy field or what is known as your Aura. Simply purchase a Sage wand at any metaphysical shop or health food store. White Sage or a combination of Sage and Sweetgrass is especially good for this.

To begin the clearing process of the room you are working in, light the fat end of the wand and let the edges of the sage stick smolder. As the ends turn bright red, blow gently on the flame and allow the smoke to curl up around you. Now walk around the room going clockwise, which is always a positive direction to go in when clearing energy. Move the smoke around doorways, around the edges of windows and mirrors, inside cabinets and drawers and all around your furniture.

I like to think of the smoke as an energetic sponge, scrubbing clean all of the walls, the windows, doors and furniture. Gently blow on the burning ends and let the smoke rise up around the entire space you are in. The smoke and the intention of clearing the space will strip away the stuck or negative energy that might reside there and prepare the room and you for the next step of calling in spirits. Now open a door or window to release any negative energy and clear the smoke from the Sage wand.

Before you put out the Sage wand, lean over and gently smudge yourself. Start at you feet and let the smoke move up your legs from your feet. Move across your belly and chest, then run the wand under your arms and up around your head.

If you have someone handy who can do your back, great, let them do the back of your body. When they have finished, smudge them as well, front and back.

If you do not have a helper, hold the wand behind you at the small of your back and let the smoke do the work; rising up behind your shoulders and neck, clearing your aura and raising your vibrations.

When you feel like you are finished with the smudging, place the smudge stick in a bowl of sand or cat litter to extinguish the flames. The wand is re-usable. When it cools you can place it in a safe place for later use.

Another method for clearing space is to use a regular spray bottle, that you would find in the garden center of the grocery store, and finely ground sea salt. Place four or five teaspoons of sea salt in the spray bottle, then fill it with warm water. Let the water dissolve the salt and then hold the bottle between your palms. Visualize white, cleansing light filling the bottle with energy. You will feel hot or cold as you do this, but don't worry it is just energy moving through you.

When you feel like you have filled the bottle with as much energy as possible, go around the room you are working in and spray, just like you would do with the smoke of the smudge stick. Spray the walls lightly with the sea salt combination, spray around your furniture, and your windows, but not *on* your windows.

Spray yourself at the end of the cleansing. Sea salt is a powerful purifier and combined with white light and water you have created a form of "Holy Water" charged and ready to cleanse anything.

If you have plants or a fish tank stay away from them with the sea salt and the Sage Wand. Salt will kill both the fish and the plants. The smoke of the sage will sometimes choke plants, especially Norfolk pines or delicate ferns.

While I was creating the mixture for this particular incense, I felt cold, shivery and a little "weird." I was aware of someone or some kind of energy watching me as I mixed the ingredients. I *knew* it was a Guide or an entity that just wanted to make contact with me, so I went with the feelings and allowed the interaction to take place.

If you feel any "weird" or uncomfortable feelings while you are mixing the following recipe, circle yourself in White Light and ask your Guides and Angels to join you. Know that the Spirit Realm is always ready to communicate with you. All you have to do is invite them in with love and light.

One last item before we start creating Spirit Calling Incense. You need to know that the Spirit Realm will not hurt you while you are doing this recipe and meditation. The only way that you will have negative results with this mixture is if you are thinking of or wanting to attract in hateful, negative spirits. I advise against this.

Do not mix this incense if you are having an especially bad day or have lots of negative emotions going on. Wait for a time when you are more focused, calmer and clear with your intent.

Last but not least, the herbs in this mixture are very watery, emotional herbs which will create strong reactions in your Heart Chakra, (The Heart Chakra is located in the middle of the chest and your Crown Chakra at the top of your head). Let these areas in your body react to the energy. It will clear out any blockages and open you up intuitively.

Now we are ready to proceed with Spirit Calling Incense.

HERBS YOU WILL NEED:

- ½ cup Blessed Thistle – Power and Spirit calling.
- ¼ cup Violet Flowers – Opens the heart to love, healing, and Spirit calling.
- ½ cup Myrrh Resin – Love, healing, and Spirit calling.
- ½ cup Mugwort – Dreams, and flying.
- ½ cup Marshmallow – Raises feminine emotion, connects to lunar energy and dreams.
- ¼ cup Cinnamon Chips – Enhances psychic power, raising vibrations, cleansing energetic blockages.

ESSENTIAL OILS YOU WILL NEED:

- 6 drops Wisteria oil – Calls in spirits.

The Violet flowers are very hard to crush. Use the blender to crush them. Don't worry if you cannot crush the flowers completely.

Blend all the herbs together. Add the Wisteria Oil one drop at a time. With each drop visualize kind and gentle Spirits coming to speak with you. When you feel like you have mixed the herbs to your desired consistency, prepare the charcoal. Focus on the Spirit Realm and those that have passed away that you loved and want to communicate with.

While the charcoal briquette heats in the incense burner, hold a pinch of the Spirit Calling Incense in your hand. Smell it. Focus on it. Pay attention to what part of your body reacts. How does that reaction feel?

If you are aware of fearful feelings coming up, release the fear by breathing in and blowing out through your mouth. Spirits will not harm you! They simply want to be acknowledged and are coming in for your highest good to give you messages that you are loved and thought of. Now listen to the sounds around you.

Spirits will speak to you through noises, not just feelings or thoughts.

Do you hear soft rapping or knocking, creaking of doors or other noises that are not usually in your environment? Those are all signals that the energetic veil that is between our world and the world of the departed has opened and they have entered into your space and are ready to communicate with you.

Other sounds you may hear include a wind chime tinkling, without a breeze to help it sing. You might feel cold or hot. Lights might flicker or you will hear a door-bell or cell phone go off with no one on the other end. It is how they communicate with us. Do not be afraid, they are confirming that you have called them in and they are with you ready to communicate.

Spirits will not create disruption unless you have intentionally invited "negative energies" to come into your personal space. If you find yourself feeling uncomfortable with the energies you have focused on, simply breathe in white light. Ask your Guides and Angels to protect you. Focus on the Spirits that you want to connect with and allow the negative energies to return to their Realm.

While the Spirit Calling incense burns on the charcoal, get comfortable either in a favorite chair or on the floor. Place another pinch of Spirit Calling incense on the charcoal. Let the aroma fill you with its divine energy. As you connect with the incense, allow your mind to think about those people who have passed. Think about the people you might have unfinished business with. Ask them to gently and lovingly come to you. Ask them to speak to your heart or simply be around your energy.

Unfinished business means having words or issues with any of your loved ones' who have passed away. Now is the time to think about those feelings and issues. You may vocalize those feelings or silently send a private message to the Spirits in the room with you.

If you are not sensing the Spirits that may be around you now, they are aware of you, and they know about your desire to connect with them. Do not be discouraged if nothing is happening. This is a learned and practiced technique. Be patient and know that at any time, those on the Other Side can return to speak with you.

I have found, when doing this work, that present time is not always when they appear to me. Later in the night, when I am fast asleep, all the things I wanted to accomplish in my meditation during the day happened while I lay peaceful without the blockage of doubt.

Spirits have come gently into my sleep, speaking very explicitly about how they are, what they are doing, and what issue I need to release between us. The meditation was simply a way to open the door and invite them into my space.

Do not be disappointed if you are not interacting right now. Continue to breathe and be open-minded about the interactions or sensations you may be experiencing.

Continue breathing White Light, in through your nose, out through your mouth. Now visualize those people you would like to connect with or simply would like to send messages to. Pay attention to how your body is reacting to this process.

Are there any new smells in the room with you? Perhaps you are noticing a specific perfume or cologne that brings back memories of your Father's Old Spice aftershave or Grandma's strong, flowery perfume?

Do you feel cold or warm? Are there prickles on the back of your neck?

Are there any sounds occurring around you that you would not normally hear in your house?

Do you have goose bumps on your arms or legs?

Do you hear knocking on the walls or tabletops around you?

Do not analyze this too much, just go with it, stay open and continue to breathe in white light. It is their way of saying "Hello I am here."

You may feel light headed, dizzy and even hypersensitive right now. It's O.K. Let it happen! If you physically "see" a spirit while you are doing this exercise, *do not be afraid!* They are just saying, "Hello" and letting you know they are with you. Communicate with them like you would communicate with an old friend, letting that Spirit know that you think of them often and miss them being in your life today. The spirit realm appreciates these things.

Think about the activities you used to do with the loved ones' who have passed on. The Spirit Realm loves to acknowledge familiar things. They enjoy sharing how much they liked drinking coffee, smoking, saying goodnight to the grandchildren or participating in church or any of the worldly pleasures they were known for while they were alive.

Release any negative feelings you may have had with those you are wishing to converse with, allowing healing to flow through you and between you. In Spirit there is no hate. There is no anger. There is only forgiveness and unconditional love. Let yourself cry or laugh, letting all your emotions come up and out. Allow yourself to experience closure and to clear any blockages in your emotional, mental and physical self.

When you feel like you have finished conversing with the spirit realm, take a deep breath of white light. Run white light through your body, clearing any negativity you may have brought up or created by calling in the Other Side. If you are experiencing any pain in your body immediately send white light to that area, releasing the pain.

Thank your Guides and Angels for protecting you. Thank those that have passed for visiting you. Now thank the Universe for allowing you to step across the veil of energy that separates us from the dead. Take a moment to continue breathing and clearing your energy again. Breathe in through your nose, bringing in cleansing white light and releasing any fear, uncomfortable feelings or pain through your breath.

Be sure to release any negative feelings or pain through your mouth by blowing it out up from your spine and through your throat and finally out of your mouth. Do this until you feel clear and pain free.

Tell the Spirits you have invited in to return gently to their own Realm in love and light. Ask for any other spirits that may have entered your personal space, to also return to their Realm in the light of unconditional love. Say this several times until you no longer feel any energies or spirits remaining in your sacred space or your body temperature has returned to normal.

Body temperature will signal that your energy and theirs have separated enough for you to move on and they have returned to their place of origin.

If you find yourself still feeling "not quite right," take a sea salt bath. Put a few tablespoons of fine sea salt in bath water, soak for about ten minutes and feel your aura cleansing as well as your body. Sea Salt is a great purifier and will clear any negative energy that might have attached to you during the meditation. Sea Salt will cleanse any "unbalanced" feelings that might have come up and brighten up your mood as well as your chakras.

Now take a moment to place your hands on the floor, palms down and connect to the ground beneath you. Hold your hands there for a few minutes, grounding your energy and connecting to Mother Earth. Touching earth balances the energy and brings you into focus again. When you feel like you are fully focused and "back in your body," package Spirit Calling incense and label it.

Log all of your reactions, feelings, insecurities and positive aspects of what you have accomplished.

You may feel "energy fluctuations" throughout the rest of the day or night. It is a normal thing to move energy after this experience. The shifting will cause you to feel hot or cold and emotionally sensitive. Let your body go with it. Honor how you feel after this exercise.

Drink lots of water and maybe eat some protein to balance out the extreme energy shifts you are now experiencing. Chocolate is another great way to balance the electrolytes and energy movement in the body. Do what feels right for you to help yourself feel grounded and focused.

If nothing happened during this exercise, do not be hard on yourself or wonder if it is "real" or not. Sometimes it is just not the right time for the interaction to occur. It may happen in the night while you are sleeping or it may happen during another meditation at another time.

Later on, you may have a deep, enriching encounter with spirits which will let you know that the healing and releasing you did worked. Everything happens when it is supposed to, especially when doing energy work. Pay attention over the next few weeks as your energy continues to evolve and open further.

You have successfully moved yourself forward by being open and receptive to the possibilities of communicating with the dead. Do not get stuck in "over analyzing" the experiences you just had. Be open-minded to it. Let the feelings and images, sounds, body reactions or thoughts sit in your awareness and flow through you.

Everything you went through in creating this recipe is part of the process of diving deeper into the Scents of your own Soul. Honor what you felt and went through, even if no communication occurred at this time.

Closing note on this chapter

In my experience, Spirits want to connect when there is closure, healing or protection that might need to happen. By protection, I mean letting you know that you are being kept very safe from harm energetically.

Spirits will come to you in a way that will grab your attention and make you notice them like a shadow flitting by you in the corner of your eye, or a ringing phone with no one on the other end of the line. Sometimes those that crossed over will rap on the wall or knock pictures over, they will make the door bell ring or play certain important music on the radio that only you would connect to, to give you messages. Lights will flicker on and off and they will interfere with electrical appliances to say hello.

Aroma is another way of connecting to you. Pay attention to any new scents that suddenly appear throughout the next few weeks after creating this incense. Smells that resonate to what a loved one wore or smoked will lightly drift up, reminding you of them. This is their way of saying "I love you."

CHAPTER SEVEN

Shaman Incense

THIS INCENSE is dedicated to Sandy, the most inspiring Shaman I have ever had the pleasure of meeting.

Definition of the word Shaman:
A priest or priestess who uses magic for the purpose of curing the sick and divining the hidden. Webster's Dictionary.

HERBS YOU WILL NEED:

- ⅛ cup Sweet grass – Lunar energy, spirit communication, and cleansing sacred space.
- ½ cup Tobacco (Crushed cigarettes are ideal) – Purifies sacred space, spirit communication, and raising vibrations.
- ¼ cup Sage – Clearing sacred space and summoning ancestors.
- 1 finely ground Tonka Bean – Inspires love, raises emotional vibrations in the body and opens the heart chakra.
- ¼ cup Myrrh Resin – Lunar energy, raises emotional awareness and brings in spirits.
- ¼ cup Elecampane – Opens the throat chakra, attracts animals and raises intuition by opening the third eye.
- ⅛ cup Benzoin Gum – Binder.

OILS YOU WILL NEED:

- 4 drops of cinnamon oil – Raises vibrations in the aura. Clears negative energy. (Caution! This oil is very irritating to the eyes and skin.)

Combine the dry ingredients. Allow the earthiness of the herbs you are mixing to grab your awareness. Tune into them. Feel Mother Earth reaching through the dried herbs to caress your arms with her strong, healing energy.

In your heart and mind, concentrate on calling in the directions of North, South, East and West. Acknowledge the vibrations of the rich earth in the North. Think of passionate fire in the South. Feel the winds of air in the East. Ride the waves of emotion with water in the West.

Invite these sacred energies to join you as you mix the ingredients. Feel the powerful energies of the directions inter- twining with your beautiful energy. Focus those magnificent energies into the herbal mixture you are creating. You may feel your hands becoming very hot while you mix and visualize.

You may also feel surges of power running through your body as you work with this mixture. Let it happen! Invite your Native American guides to come into your space and fill the incense with the energy of the elders. You do not need to know who those guides might be; just know that they are around because you asked them to join you in the process.

Focus on how the sensations in your body are changing and rising up through you.

When you are finished mixing, charge the Shaman Incense by lifting the bowl of freshly made incense above your head. Face the direction, North. Say out loud, "I ask for the blessings of the North – wisdom, Mother Earth, mighty trees and stable rocks – to fill my body and this recipe with your energy."

Feel mother Earth beneath you, pulsing and creating strength in your spine.

Turn to the East. Raise the bowl above your head. Say out loud, "I ask for the bless- ings of the East – brilliant sun, illumination, spiritual challenges and new begin- nings – to fill my body and this recipe with your energy."

You may feel light and a bit "out of your body" as the energies of the East come in light and free.

Turn to the South. Raise the bowl above your head. Say out loud, "I ask for the blessings of the South – passion, warmth, trust, childlike energies and transformation – to fill my body and this incense recipe."

You may experience surges of heat moving through you or even sweating while performing this part of the ceremony.

Face West. Lift the bowl above your head. Say out loud, "I ask for the blessings of the West – lakes, mighty oceans and streams, emotional cleansing, love and compassion – to flow through my body and into this incense recipe."

You may feel like weeping or become heavy hearted. Allow all the various feelings and sensations to move through you while charging the incense. You are moving energy, energies that are vital to us but forgotten in our everyday lives. Connect to them!

Now we will bring in the final energy to charge this incense. Lift the bowl of incense above your head one last time. Stand straight and look up.

Say out loud, "I ask for the blessings of Great Spirit to charge this incense and my body. I ask for the blessings of Father Sky, Sister Moon and Mother Earth to touch my heart. I ask for healing and connection to all the beauty of the earth to come into my life. Fill this incense with your transformative energies."

Light the Charcoal and place it in the incense burner. When the charcoal is hot and the energies you invited in are vibrating through your body, take a pinch of incense from the bowl and place it on the charcoal. Feel the strength of the incense filling your home and your senses. Sit in the energy, letting your mind wander.

Feel the earth beneath you. Pay close attention to the sensations running through you. Breathe deeply in through your nose and out through your mouth, as you allow the energy of Mother Earth to lend you strength, wisdom, and the ability to shift directions in your life. Feel the surges of watery energy moving inside you, allowing the emotional balance to swim with change and drive, swiftly moving through this energetic transformation.

Sit and breathe. Let your energy and the energies that were called on cleanse and fill your body, completely, opening to the Universe and all it holds for you.

When you are finished, thank Mother Earth and Father Sky for their wisdom and their blessings. Get a large glass of water; eat some chocolate or protein to replenish your body. Bag the mixture and label it. Be sure to log what you experienced as the shaman of your own life.

CHAPTER 8

Raven Incense

THIS RECIPE is a favorite of mine because through much of my life, Ravens have been a familiar visitor to my home. They are the keeper of secrets, the messengers of the dark of night, and the animal totem of the dead.

Ravens assist in accessing your own personal freedom to soar through this world into the next. They encourage us to leave our earthly bodies behind, flying into personal transcendence.

Raven Incense is an aromatically beautiful recipe and my version of an astral projection tool to be used when meditating or dreaming.

HERBS YOU WILL NEED:

- ½ cup Frankincense Resin - Power, clearing sacred space, raising vibrations.
- ¼ cup Myrrh Resin - Opens the heart chakra and raises emotional awareness, clears sacred space, opens the crown chakra.
- ⅛ cup Mistletoe - Attracts animal energies, raises healing vibrations in the body, lends energetic protection.
- ½ cup Cinnamon Chips - Opens the heart chakra, clears sacred space and raises vibrations in the human aura.
- ¼ cup Angelica - Stimulates the crown chakra, enhances visions and dreams, and lends energetic power.
- ½ cup Benzoin Gum – Binder.
- 1 Charcoal briquette crushed. (Use the kind of charcoal designed for burning in incense burners such as Swift Light or Three Kings charcoal briquettes).

OILS YOU WILL NEED:

- 8 drops Lavender oil – Soothes the nervous system, opens the heart center.
- 8 drops Lotus oil – Connects the body's energies to the Universal healing energies.

Mix the ingredients slowly as you focus your attention on the way the herbs feel in your hands. How does the resin feel?

Pay attention to the sensations you may be experiencing in your shoulder blades and neck. Your heart might be racing as you crush and grind this mixture, yet don't be alarmed; it is merely your energy rising with the combinations of the herbal mixture.

You may have the sensation of feeling like a bird, a mighty Raven, ready to take off at a moment's notice. You may hear more birds than usual outside your home or you may have images of birds in your mind's eye as you mix this incense. Let the transition happen, paying close attention to how your body feels.

Become aware of the pressure in your shoulder blades as you add the lavender oil to the mix. If nothing is happening, don't worry, it will. Breathe in the fragrant aroma of the Lavender. Let it relax and assist you in connecting to the energy of mysticism and vision.

Your Third Eye, the psychic center of the body, is slowly opening. A small amount of pressure in the center of your forehead might occur. Allow it to happen, this is a normal reaction to the herbal mixture. If the sensations in your forehead or shoulders are too intense or uncomfortable, simply touch the floor with your hands and connect to the earth. This will ground you and bring you back into your body.

When you are ready add the Lotus oil *slowly*. Feel the energies in the incense mixture amplifying. Let your body drift into the powerful awareness of the Raven, the sacred, mystical creature of Shamans.

Raven being invited into your life opens the gates between this world and the world of Spirit. Place a pinch of Raven incense onto the charcoal and gently inhale the scent. Let the energy envelope around you as your personal energy opens further. Now ask the energies of Raven to join you and quietly open up your heart and mind.

Sister Raven will share her insights into the transformations you desire in your current situations. Do not disregard any thoughts or images you may be experiencing right now. Raven is a visual energy that will lend you her insights if you ask for them.

Raven's subtle voice will show you images and give you messages. She will inspire you to delve deeper into your own spiritual beliefs. She will connect you to questions about the dead or any secrets you may need to release or see through. Trust her and pay attention to your own reactions to this incredible energy.

When you feel like you have finished speaking with Raven, take a deep breath and ask Raven to share the experience of feeling wings sprouting from your shoulder blades. Place another pinch of incense on the charcoal and inhale gently. Feel pressure behind your shoulder blades as the energy of Raven melds with your energy.

If this sensation is too intense or uncomfortable for you, again touch the ground with your palms to ground out the sensations and focus your energy back to your body.

If you feel comfortable meshing your energy with Raven energy, ask Sister Raven to let you join her on an adventure in your mind, flying high above the world and riding the winds of night. Let her float in and out of your thoughts. Feel her airy, mystical energies showing you how to spread your own beautiful wings and join her in flying to the top of your dreams and inspirations.

When you feel like you are finished communing with Raven, take a deep breath of White Light in through your nose. Send the white light into your shoulder blades, releasing the energy of Sister Raven from your shoulder blades.

Breathe in white light through your nose and send it through your body, down to your toes and out to the floor. Touch the floor with your palms, grounding out the sensations of flying in your mind and body. Visualize a bubble of brilliant Gold Light all around you, encapsulating your aura.

Sit in this energy for a few moments longer. Be aware of your mind and body becoming more focused and grounded. Come back to your body and into the room you are working in.

*Drink a large glass of water or sports drink and eat some dark chocolate.
This will again balance your body and ground you. Out-of-body work
will burn up the same amount of energy as working out for two hours, so
replenish to stay healthy.*

When you are finished with this process, label and bag the Raven incense. Log your feelings, your reactions and any messages you may have received.

Be aware that the next few weeks may bring Sister Raven's blessings to you, connecting you to the actual bird and all its mysticism and knowledge. She will happily bring you messages from the night, during sleep time or in your daydreams about your mystical self.

Be sure to thank Sister Raven for her insight into the secrets of your Soul.

CHAPTER 9

The Chakra System

NOW that you have a basic understanding of energy and a general feel for what it is like working with the incense recipes, I would like to wake your body up even more by working with the Chakra system.

If you are not familiar with the Chakras, you will find the mixtures in the next chapters helpful in connecting you to the unique and divine energy centers in your body.

While working through the following recipes, you will become acutely aware of how your body feels energetically and what blockages reside in your chakra system that keep you from being the best you can be in your life. If you are a seasoned Chakra worker, you will find the aromas, herbs, essential oils and meditations very helpful in further awakening your energy.

If you are new to working with the Chakras, go slow at first and take time to process the emotions, sensations and issues that may come up while creating the recipes and working through the meditations.

Every human body is made up of energy. We circulate that energy or electrical current through our bodies, giving our energy to others, bringing in energy from others and replenishing our own energy. These energy centers are referred to as Chakras.

The word Chakra (pronounced Shock – ra or Chock – ra) means wheel or disk in Sanskrit. A Chakra is thought to be a wheel of spinning light that is invisible to the average human eye.

Definitions of the Chakras

The Chakras begin at the base of the Spine.

The FIRST or BASE CHAKRA represents survival, fear issues, Kundalini or sexually based energy. It is also the place that we hold old hurts and abuse issues. This is where you received love and affection and it is also the place where abuse and survival skills sit.

It is the grounding energy of the earth and the stability of being connected to earth. It is the place of strength and power or survival and weakness.

The SECOND CHAKRA is located below the navel and above the pelvic bone. This Chakra represents pro-creation, creativity and attraction. This is where you hold desire for sex, friends, material possessions, power and God/Goddess. It is the center for fertility in all that you do and the energy of being sexual.

The THIRD CHAKRA resides between the Solar plexus, in the middle of the rib cage. The THIRD CHAKRA is the power center of the body. It represents your ego, personal power issues, and self-esteem. It is the root of gut-level intuition and the source of motivation or lack of self.

The FOURTH CHAKRA is located between the chest and collarbone. This Chakra rules the heart, unconditional love, truth, giving, heartaches, and fears of receiving or giving love. It is the place where we open to others and accept each person for who they are as well as accepting ourselves.

The FIFTH CHAKRA is located in the center of the collarbone at the base of the throat. It represents communication, creativity and spirituality.

The SIXTH CHAKRA is located in the middle of the forehead. This is referred to as the Third Eye or Intuitive Center of the body. It represents metaphysical knowledge and higher intuition.

The SEVENTH CHAKRA resides in the top of the head, known as the CROWN CHAKRA. This Chakra opens up the Aura to receive the Higher Power of God's Light. The Seventh Chakra connects you to Higher Power, Angels and Guides.

The human body also contains Chakras in the palm of the hands, the middle of the feet, the knees, and the back of the neck. They are also around the outer edges of the Aura, known as the Etheric Body. Studies have discovered at least 32 Chakras throughout the human body.

In this book, we will only be working with the Seven Chakras.

The exercises in the following pages are designed to move energy from the base of the spine, the First Chakra to the Outer Aura. I recommend doing these in order if you have never worked with the Chakras. If you are familiar with and work with them on a consistent basis; then skipping around to what is appropriate for you is encouraged.

Colors For Breathwork

In energy work, breath is an important element in moving blockages that might be in the various Chakras. Simple, focused breathing opens up the vibrations of the body and is a quick, easy way to shift your awareness to the Chakra System. Each color resonates to the individual Chakras, starting at the base of the spine and working up to the top of the head and the outer Aura.

By breathing in through your nose and out through the mouth while visualizing the corresponding colors of the Chakra System you create a movement of energy which flows and radiates throughout the body. Listed below are the corresponding colors to each Chakra.

BASE CHAKRA: Located at the base of the spine. Breathe in red right up through the nose and release. Move the colors up and down the spine by breathing red in through the nose and blowing out hard through the mouth.

SECOND CHAKRA: Located between the pelvic bone and navel. Breathe in orange light through the nose, releasing and moving the colors red, black or white up through the spine and through the mouth. Black energy moving up the spine is negative energy being released. You may use white for this if you prefer a gentler release.

THIRD CHAKRA: Located in the Solar Plexus. Breathe in yellow or gold light through your nose, moving the colors black or red up from the base of the spine and out through the mouth. Blow out red to remove anger that will interfere with your personal power center. Blow out black to release negativity from your lower chakras.

FOURTH CHAKRA: Located above the breastbone between the throat and the chest. Breathe in green light or pink light through the nose and move the colors red or black, up from the base of the spine blowing out through the mouth.

FIFTH CHAKRA: Located at the base of the throat. Breathe in blue light, move the colors black or red up from the base of the spine and blow hard out of the mouth releasing negativity.

SIXTH CHAKRA: Located in the middle of the forehead. Known as The Third Eye. Breathe in purple or indigo light through your nose and move the colors red or black up from the base of the spine and out of your mouth.

SEVENTH CHAKRA: Located at the top of your head, known as The Crown Chakra. Breathe in White Light sending it to the top of your head. Blow out through your mouth any negative feelings you have while White Light is moving up through your crown.

CHAPTER 10

First Chakra – Incense & Meditation

HERBS YOU WILL NEED:

- 1 root Galangal, ground – Attracts money, clears anger and negativity, raises positive vibrations and aids in healing.
- ½ cup Fennel – Aids in protecting the body and attracting stability, wealth and balance.
- 2 tsps. Allspice – Resonates to the first chakra, creating healing and balance in the body.
- ½ cup Cinnamon Chips – Raises energies in the body, opens the first chakra.
- ⅛ cup Copal Resin - Clears negative energies in the body.
- 1Tbls. Benzoin Gum - Binder
- ¼ cup Pine Sawdust – Filler (This is optional in all the Incense recipes. You may use it to give the mixture more volume or use only the herbs as they are suggested.)

ESSENTIAL OILS YOU WILL NEED:

- 6 drops Rosemary oil – Opens All the chakras, clears negative energy and encourages healing in the body.
- 4 drops Red Food Coloring (Red represents the first chakra… this is optional).

The First Chakra or the Base Chakra is considered to be the beginning of your energy centers. In this spot, located at the base of the tailbone, we hold the energy of beginnings, survival, energetic grounding, and Mother Earth, rebirth and abuse issues. In our day-to-day life the Base Chakra is flared continually as we attempt to survive, stay focused and be supported in the world.

We often feel anger with other people, frustration with our money flow, and perhaps feel like we cannot get ahead in our careers. We generally feel let down by our relationships and even often wonder why the Universe itself has forgotten us. These deep emotions can create hip and buttocks pain, especially if we are feeling a lack of support in our everyday endeavors.

Whatever issues may be lodged in your First Chakra will rapidly be brought up and consequently released with First Chakra Incense. You may feel back pain or uneasy feelings in your lower spine as you create this recipe. Just go with it. Let yourself breathe through the discomfort, keeping in mind that you are moving deep, emotional energy blocks up and out of your spine. Be aware that First Chakra Incense will also release the emotion of anger.

DO NOT burn this Incense when other people around you are not doing First Chakra work !!

First Chakra Incense will create arguments, violence and unhappy moods for those who are not aware of what you are doing with the mix. With that, let's get started on working the Chakras!

Take a few deep cleansing breaths in through your nose and out through your mouth. Become aware of any anxiety you may be feeling in the body, especially in your lower back. With each deep breath in, send white light down your spine. Feel it. Know it. See it as you fill your spine with beautiful white spirit light.

Now go ahead and grind the Galangal root. (Try a carrot grater for this task, it works great!) Visualize prosperity coming to you with each stroke of the grater.

Galangal Root is the key to opening up the First Chakra to prosperity.

Add the rest of the dried herbs to the Galangal and as you crush the herbs, pay attention to how you are feeling. If you are experiencing anger or harsh feelings in your spine, breathe in white light again, sending it down to your tail bone. This will help to clear the uncomfortable feelings you are experiencing and allow you to concentrate on making the blend.

When I created this incense, I felt angry, fearful and sad. I experienced fierce emotions as I crushed the herbs and actually had to go outside and stomp my feet, releasing the emotions that were coming up in my body. It took me quite off guard and made me realize how potent the combination truly was.

When all the herbs have been mixed together, grind them in the blender to create a fine powder. Add the Rosemary oil slowly and relax into your feelings with each drop of the oil. Rosemary oil is a extremely strong, reactionary oil. It can bring up childhood memories, and feelings of anger, earthiness and old hurts. Let the emotions flow through you, acknowledging them and claiming them as your own.

If you are experiencing pain in your back, breathe through it and send white light into your body to release any negativity.

Add the food coloring directly to the blend, letting the colors seep into the herbs. Add as much or as little as you wish, depending on how intense you would like the red to become.

Log how you felt while mixing the First Chakra Incense, in your journal, being explicit about any body pains or anger that came up for you.

First Chakra Meditation

Pre-record the following meditation and prepare a quiet, sacred space for you to connect to your First Chakra.

Sit comfortably in a chair or on the floor, allowing your body to fully relax. Breathe in through your nose and out through your mouth. Feel any tension in your neck and shoulders releasing as you inhale and exhale. (*Pause.*)

Let your back and arms relax, breathing in and then breathing out. (*Pause.*)

Let your hips and legs relax, feeling the muscles in your chest, stomach and abdomen relax as well. Take a few deep breaths in through your nose and out through your mouth. (*Pause.*)

Visualize red light coming up through the floor or your chair. See it, know it and feel it moving through your legs, up past your ankles, into your knees, up through your hips and finally resting in the base of your spine. Become aware of Mother Earth filling the base of your spine with her energy. (*Pause.*)

Visualize bright, fiery red light moving clockwise around the base of your spine. Feel it moving slowly, spinning gently in the Base Chakra. Take a deep breath in through your nose and release the breath through your mouth visualizing a stream of black coming up from the base of your spine, moving up your back and out of your mouth. (*Pause.*)

Breathe in again through your nose and repeat the black light moving up through the spine and out of your mouth. Blow it out hard through your mouth, releasing the energetic blockages that sit in your Base Chakra. (*Pause.*)

Focus on the red spinning Wheel of Light moving around your tailbone. Speed up the spinning, letting the energy of Red move clockwise in and out of your spine.

Let any pain, anger, sadness, or frustration dissolve away into the floor as you release your breath and let the energy move. (*Pause.*)

Look at the patterns you create that stop you from feeling supported by others. Look at how you create situations that impair your ability to make money. Pay attention to the people, things, situations and habits that keep you from being the most prosperous person you can possibly be. (*Pause.*)

See and feel those different patterns. Inhale and exhale, as you remind yourself that you would like to attract new situations. You want to create new patterns to attract bountiful supplies of prosperity, support, and foundation for making money. (*Pause.*)

Feel the red light getting brighter and brighter as you tell yourself in your mind about the ways you can change the situations that are stopping you or not supporting you. You know what those changes are; allow your subconscious to acknowledge those changes. Breathe in and out as you feel, acknowledge and honor the feelings you are experiencing.

Focus on the red light that is moving through your tail bone. It is flowing in and out of your spine and then back into it, all the while getting warmer and warmer as you continue to breathe and visualize. (*Pause.*)

Gently feel the red light beginning to dissolve into the ground, releasing any residual tension, pain, sadness, anger or frustration into the floor. (*Pause*)

Breathe in through your nose and out through your mouth very slowly. Put your hands on the ground and let yourself slowly come back to the present time. Sit for a moment and become aware of the room you are working in. (*Pause*)

Stand and stretch your body, letting your energy continue to balance out. When you feel like you have fully come back to being grounded, log your experiences.

You did amazing work with this meditation and recipe mixing! Give yourself a treat. Reward yourself with a wonderful Sea Salt bath. Put a tablespoon or two of sea salt (Iodized or Dead Sea Salts) in your bathwater and soak, clearing out any residual energetic sludge on your body and in your Aura. Sparkle up your energy and know that today, you became a lighter, more radiant person who can be stable and supported in times of adversity.

CHAPTER 11

Second Chakra – Incense & Meditation

HERBS YOU WILL NEED:

- ¼ cup Banana Peel dried (You can dry the peels in the microwave or low set oven) – Creates feelings of being fertile, resonates to the second chakra, stimulates the sex organs.
- ¼ cup Bladderwrack – Releases negativity from the heart and second chakras.
- ½ cup Catnip – Inspires creativity, soothes the nervous system, creates feelings of sexiness.
- 2 Tsp. Dragon's Blood Resin – Increases personal power, opens the base and second chakra.
- 1 Tbls. Benzoin Gum - Binder.

ESSENTIAL OILS YOU WILL NEED:

- 4 drops Essential Dragon's blood oil (make sure when purchasing Dragon's Blood oil it is not a perfume base. If it is, it will stink when you burn it). Raises the potency of the herbs and oils in the recipe.
- 1 ½ tsps.Olive Oil – Increases the libido.
- 5 drops Orange Oil – Opens the second and Fourth Chakra to feelings of accepting love.
- 5 drops Ylang Ylang oil – Heightens sexual sensations in the lower chakras.

Second Chakra Incense is designed to open the energy center that lies between the navel and your pelvis. This center governs creativity, sexuality, reproduction and sexual attraction. The color that represents this center is orange.

The herbs you will be mixing in this recipe, all raise these kinds of vibrations After completing the mixing process of this Incense, I found myself wanting to redecorate my house, buy new clothes with a whole different style to them, and completely revamp what I looked like. I felt incredibly sexual as I mixed up this recipe. You may experience all these varied emotions.

Mix the Banana Peel, Catnip and Bladderwrack together by hand or in a blender. (The Bladderwrack is a difficult herb to crush by hand; it works much better in the blender.) Add the Dragon's Blood Powder and Benzoin Gum Powder. As you combine these herbs together, visualize yourself feeling very earthy, lusty or sexy, creative and wonderfully powerful.

Pay attention to how your body feels as you mix the herbs and reveal these emotions about yourself.

Add the Hawthorne Berries. *Do not crush them.* Hawthorne Berries have higher energy in their original form as opposed to being crushed. Mix all the herbs together. Feel your own sexual energy rise with each stir of the pestle. You may feel hot at the base of your spine, let it happen! Feel the sensations rising up your spine. It is opening up your divinely, beautiful energy!

Begin adding the oils. With each drop of oil, ask your Guides and Angels to bring in "higher creative energy". Ask your Guides and Angels to open up your second chakra, very gently, with every drop of oil. Remember to breathe through this process. You may feel some uncomfortable body sensations occurring. Just go with it and breathe!

Mix the herbs and oils until you feel comfortable with the texture and smell. Test it on the charcoal, inhaling through your nose and out through your mouth as you hold your hands, palms down, over the mixture.

Now see, feel and know Orange Light is streaming in through your hands and down into the mixture. Think about filling this recipe with creative energy and passion. Think about the energy of attraction and send that into the mix as well. If you are happy with the way the incense feels, get ready to meditate. If not, add a little more Orange oil and Ylang Ylang oil. These two oils mask the bitterness of the Catnip and Bladderwrack.

Log how you felt while mixing the Second Chakra Incense. Did you feel sexiness stirring inside of you? Were you distracted by the way your house or office looks or feels? Did you want to look at yourself in the mirror and examine your current looks? Did you feel uncomfortable or "full" in your abdomen or did you feel nothing at all? Pay attention to these reactions by logging them and then looking at them after the meditation. It will clue you in to how your second chakra is working, if it is working at all, or blocked.

Second Chakra Meditation

Pre- record this meditation, playing soft, earthy music that will enhance your creativity.

YOU WILL NEED:

- An orange taper candle,
- A candle holder,
- A charcoal briquette
- An incense holder
- A pencil and paper.

Sit in a comfortable position in a chair or on the floor. Close your eyes. Take a few deep cleansing breaths. Inhale through your nose and out through your mouth. Let any aches or pains in your body, blow out through your cleansing breaths. *(Pause.)*

As you take the next cleansing breath in, visualize white light going in through your nose and down through your body. Allow divine white light to spread down to your toes. When you are ready, bring the white light up around the outside of your body like a big sleeping blanket of light. The white light will cleanse your Aura, sparkle it up and remove negativity from your energy. Take another deep breath and release slowly through your mouth.

Release any tension you may be feeling in your neck, shoulders and arms while breathing in and out. Allow the worries of the day to dissolve away into the floor. Let your mind begin to wander. *(Pause.)*

Let your back, arms, and legs relax. Allow your chest to relax as you take a deep breath in. Hold it. Release the breath. *(Pause.)*

Allow your stomach muscles to relax. *(Pause.)*

Visualize, feel and know bright Orange light. If you have trouble visualizing this, see the word orange in your mind and feel it moving up your legs and past your buttocks. Feel the energy of Orange light moving past your hips and up through the base of your spine. Move it up to the spot between your navel and your pubic bone. Allow the Orange light to sit in your abdomen as you breathe in through your nose and out through your mouth. *(Pause.)*

Begin to visualize, see and feel the energy of orange light moving gently in your abdomen, spinning clockwise as you breathe in through your nose and out through your mouth. Let any pain or discomfort you may be experiencing dissolve away into the floor. (Pause.)

Let your mind wander to the places where you have allowed your creativity to shut down. Visualize the creative goals, desires and situations you want to have around you, but have not allowed in for whatever reason. (Pause.)

Now pay attention to what may be blocking you from moving forward with those projects. As you become aware of these energy blocks, blow out through your mouth the patterns that are keeping your creatively stuck. (Pause.)

Let your mind go to the things you desire. Think about what you want to attract. Visualize those things and imagine them getting closer to you as you continue to breathe in through your nose and out through your mouth. (Pause.)

If you feel the people in your life are blocking you from being the creative person you are, visualize those people standing in front of you. Pay attention to how you feel about them.

Are you experiencing pain or discomfort in your pelvic area as you feel their presence? (Pause.)

See the people who are causing you pain or discomfort standing before you, circled in pink unconditional love light. Wrap these people in pink bubbles of light. Inhale deeply and blow out hard through your mouth, releasing them to the Universe in love and light. Let go of the pain or discomfort. (Pause.)

Feel the *orange* light that is spinning in your abdomen, picking up speed and moving clockwise in and out of your abdomen. The orange light is becoming brighter and shinier. You feel the energy of it moving in and out of your second chakra. As the orange light becomes radiantly bright, feel it slowing down, stopping and finally resting in your abdomen.

Breathe in through your nose and out through your mouth, becoming aware of your breath and how deep it sounds. Feel the floor or chair beneath you and how warm or cold your body is right now. Become aware of your fingers and toes. Wiggle them as you gently and slowly begin to open your eyes. Come all the way back to the room you are in. Breathe in and out gently, allowing yourself to stretch your arms and come fully back.

When you feel fully grounded and are all the way back from the meditation, write down the goals and aspirations that you would like to attain, on a piece of paper. *Be explicit about these goals, even if they are whimsical.* Light the orange taper candle and place it in the candleholder. Light the charcoal and place it in the incense burner. When the charcoal is hot (it will be gray around the edges) put a pinch of second chakra Incense on the charcoal.

Think about what you wrote on the piece of paper. How can you move to reach the goals you have written down? Visualize the answer to this question then see yourself moving forward with every thing you wrote down. Burn the piece of paper over the orange candle, again visualizing your goals and desires being sent to the Universe. Put the ashes from the piece of paper in a pan. Take the pan outside and release the ashes to the Universe, making your intentions and desires known. Come back inside.

Put a few drops of Dragon's Blood oil and a tablespoon of Sea Salt into a nice warm bath. Soak for as long as you can, but if you are pressed for time five minutes is plenty of time to let the energies settle in the body.

You did a great job! Now you are wide open to create, create, create! Log your feelings, reactions, and experiences in your journal, paying attention to how you felt while doing the meditation. Did you feel stuck? How were you stuck?

What patterns do you create to sabotage your creativity and creation abilities? Did you feel stuck sexual energy or was your sexual energy magnified while doing the meditation? How did you feel releasing the people in your life that create stagnation or creative conflict for you? What goals did you set regarding your career, creativity or new projects?

Write it all down and watch your creative energy and manifestation talents emerge in the following weeks. Treat yourself to some chocolate and be sure to rehydrate yourself after this work. You are a beautiful creatrix of energy!

CHAPTER 12

Third Chakra Incense

The Third Chakra is located between the Solar Plexus, where the rib cage meets the breast bone. It is the center of your personal power. It governs feeling powerful or defeated. The third Chakra signals conflict in the body…you know, that tight upset stomach feeling that says, "This isn't quite right. It doesn't feel good." That weird, little nagging in the center of your Solar Plexus is the body's sensitive alarm system going off. The color that co-ordinates to the Third Chakra is the vibrant hue of yellow.

This incense is designed to bring personal power and energy into the Third Chakra through smell. If at anytime during the mixing of this incense you feel nauseous, just breathe in white light to help balance the energy fluctuations; and know it's your power chakra trying to open and move out any unnecessary blockages.

HERBS YOU WILL NEED:

- ¼ cup Blessed Thistle – Increases feelings of personal power and strength.
- ¼ cup Rosemary – Creates harmony and strength in ALL the chakras. Amplifies intuition.
- ¼ cup Peppermint – Stimulates feelings of personal power and love for self.
- ¼ cup Cinnamon Chips – Heightens positive vibrations in the body, opens the third chakra.
- ⅛ cup Sandalwood, ground – Releases negativity, opens the chakras, balances the nervous system.
- ⅛ cup Benzoin Gum – Binder
- 3 or 4 Dried Marigold Flower tops – Instills personal power in the body.

OILS YOU WILL NEED:

- 5 drops Lemon oil – Opens the third chakra, clears negative energy and increases feeling of happiness.
- 5 drops Dragon's Blood Oil – Creates a feeling of strength and power in the body.
- 5 drops or more Yellow Food Coloring (optional)

Adding dried Marigold flowers to this mixture infuses huge amounts of power and energy to the recipe. Marigolds are a bitter smelling flower, but the energy from the plant can be felt the minute you add them.

Mix the herbs. Do you feel the intense energy that is coming from the combination? Go with it. If you feel overwhelmed, rest a moment, inhale yellow light through your nose, and send it down to your solar plexus. Let the energy settle as you work on the mixture.

The sesame seeds do not need to be crushed for they maintain their energy better, whole. Add the oils, feeling your own energies react to the aroma of the liquid.

Dragon's Blood is a very strong oil. It brings in protection, power, fiery and passionate emotions. Dab a little Dragon's Blood on the pulse points of your body, such as the neck, wrists and Third Chakra when you have to be in situations that require you to be assertive or strong.

When you have finished mixing the incense, place your hands, palms down, over the mixing bowl. Close your eyes for a moment and check how your stomach is feeling. Are you experiencing strong, assertive, energized feelings? Are you feeling like you can take on the world? Are you feeling weak, upset, unsure of yourself and generally sick to your stomach?

If you answered, "Yes" to the latter part of this question, then take a moment to inhale yellow light. Breathe in "Power" light through your nose and direct it into your Third Chakra in the solar plexus. Let the light linger there a moment. Are you aware of the energy of power moving around in your body? How does it feel?

Now take a moment to reflect on who might be in your life that brings up feelings of being powerless. (Pause here.) Who gives you a sense of being "not good enough" in their eyes? Do you have feelings of not being sure of yourself or confident in who you are? Where do those feelings come from? (*Pause.*)

See that person standing in front of you. *You might see yourself or another person, but let it happen.* Take another deep breath of yellow light. In your mind or speaking out loud, tell that person how they make you feel, even if it is yourself that needs to be told.

See yourself taking your own personal power back for your highest good by simply expressing your feelings of powerlessness. Speak the words in love and light. Feel the strength in your stomach as you claim your feelings. Own those feelings and honor the energy behind the words. *(Pause.)*

Pay attention to how you are feeling. Do you still feel unsure of yourself? Do you feel sick to your stomach? If so, take another deep breath of yellow light. Send the light again to your Third Chakra. Ask yourself why you are feeling this way? Look at the reason. Bring that reason or pattern before you.

Visualize yourself taking back your own power, saying whatever needs to be said or doing whatever it is that will correct your own lack of personal power. If you cannot find the reason for feeling powerless, continue to breathe in yellow light. Your Guides and Angels will bring you the answers to these feelings at a more appropriate time.

When you feel ready, ground yourself and take a deep breath of white light. Shake out your hands beside you, releasing any negative feelings you may be experiencing through your fingertips.

Touch the floor with your hands and take a moment longer to ground yourself.

Log your feelings and experiences with this recipe. Package the Third Chakra Incense, knowing that today you took your personal power to a new level, honoring your own strength in who you are.

This Incense is designed to assist you in those times of feeling powerless and not knowing how to take your power back. I use this Incense frequently when I am experiencing a lot of chaos in my life. Chaos tends to lead to emotional disruption which can shut down your Third Chakra. Practicing this short meditation while mixing Third Chakra Incense or burning, it can help clarify where the confusion lies. It can assist in giving clarity in how to regain "power" over the situation.

CHAPTER 13

Fourth Chakra – Incense & Meditation

THE FOURTH CHAKRA is the key to your Soul. It is the point in the human energy system which regulates your path in life and how you will achieve "soul fulfillment." It is the guide to how you will deal with the lessons you must learn before you can evolve into your Soul's path. I have felt the pain of the heart chakra in so many of my clients, friends, family, and of course myself.

It is a hard energy to deal with and a harder energy to release, leading to heart disease, high blood pressure, arterial clogging and severe heart related health issues. These conditions often stem from the energy blockages in the Fourth Chakra which are closed, shattered, wounded or protected.

Over the past ten years, I have had the privilege of observing the healing powers of the human heart. I have been witness to clients going to chakra healers who opened up the vital energy of the heart center. Through emotional cleansing, clarifying and soul retrieval, the heart center gently opened. It allowed the client to receive unconditional love and opening of the vital heart energy.

Those clients who were in need of bypass surgery or arterial reconstruction found they healed faster by opening up the heart chakra. After the healing to open the heart chakra, the clients became clearer with their feelings and allowed themselves to learn to love themselves again, and recovered quicker from their ailments.

On the other hand, I have also been witness to clients who refused to open the heart chakra, denying their own feelings and disliking everything about themselves. They ultimately did not allow others to care for them at all. This often led to an early demise, through heart attacks, arterial blockages in the heart, high cholesterol, and strokes.

As you prepare to create Fourth Chakra Incense, take a few moments to think about how you open your heart Chakra. *You may want to write down the issues that keep you in a space of not loving yourself and others.*

Consider the walls of protection you may put around your heart to keep from getting hurt. Pay attention to the hurts that may already reside in your heart chakra that have not been addressed or released. All of these issues, in some way, will block the heart chakra.

We will be clearing these emotional issues during the Fourth Chakra meditation and beginning the process of opening the heart while mixing Fourth Chakra incense.

HERBS YOU WILL NEED:

- ½ cup Patchouli – Brings feelings of "earthy" love and passion up in the emotions.
- ½ cup Rosehips - not ground – Attracts Angels and unconditional love.
- ½ cup Rose petals. (Set aside a ¼ cup) – Opens the heart chakra.
- ¼ cup Cloves – Heightens intuition and clears negativity.
- 1 cup Licorice – Inspires feelings of love and passion.
- ¼ cup Star Anise – Boosts vibrations in the body. Creates happiness.

OILS YOU WILL NEED:

- 5 drops Peppermint oil – Inspires feelings of love.
- 4 drops Patchouli oil – Stimulates the body creating feelings of love.
- 5 drops Rose oil – Clears and opens the heart chakra.
- 6 drops Green food coloring (optional)

Mix the dried ingredients, leaving some of the Rose Petals whole to add to the incense when you have completed mixing. Pay attention to your body as you mix the dried herbs. Do you have heart burn? Do you feel pressure in your chest? If so, it is your body letting you know that you are reacting to the mixture of herbs. Let those various body reactions come up. Be sure to breathe through them, releasing any discomfort.

Add the oils, again paying attention to the way your heart chakra is reacting. (The heart chakra is located in the middle of your chest above the breast and below the throat). If you are experiencing continued discomfort in the heart area, take a few deep breaths of green light. Breathe in through your nose and send the green light down into the heart center. Let the light linger for a few seconds, releasing the breath through the mouth. Do this several times until your heart area feels settled. Log your reactions, paying close attention to your body sensations as you record your thoughts and feelings.

Fourth Chakra Meditation

Pre-record soft, healing music with this meditation, such as Steven Halpern's *Angel Love* to let you fully relax and open your heart.

YOU WILL NEED:

- A green taper candle
- A candle holder
- Fourth Chakra Incense
- A charcoal Briquette
- An incense burner

To begin the meditation, find a comfortable place to sit on the floor or in a soft chair. Close your eyes. Take a few cleansing breaths, inhaling through the nose and blowing out through the mouth. Visualize green light, coming in through your nose and moving down your body. Fill the chest area with magnificent emerald green light. Breathe out any discomfort, blowing the breath hard out through your mouth. *(Pause.)*

Let the green light flow in and out of your chest area, as you become aware of the heart chakra opening up. Take another deep breath of green light, again sending it to the middle of your chest. Let your body fully relax as you open up to the energies of unconditional love and healing. *(Pause.)*

Pay attention to how you are reacting to the loving energy coming into your body. If you feel pain in any part of your body, go into the pain. Really feel the pain. Pay attention to the first thought that comes into your mind. Where is the discomfort coming from? Is it from your own emotional hurts? Is it coming from somewhere else? Let these thoughts form in front of you. *(Pause.)*

When you have clarified where the discomfort is coming from, take a deep breath in through the nose and expel it out through the mouth releasing the pain. Inhale a deep breath of green light and send that breath into your heart area. Imagine green light as a beautiful, loving embrace from your Guides and Angels. Feel the energies of your Guides and Angels all around you. They are ready to assist you in opening up your heart. *(Pause.)*

How are you feeling? Are you aware of your Guides and Angels or a presence in the room with you? Pay attention to your reactions as you release any discomfort with a cleansing breath from the mouth. *(Pause.)*

Invite your Guides and Angels to show you or give you any messages about their love and your loving path in this life. (Pause.)

If you do not receive an immediate response, don't worry, it will appear to you at a more appropriate time.

Take a moment to visualize the people who are important in your life. They are standing in front of you. How is your heart reacting to this? Release any discomfort with the breath, blowing out hard through the mouth and ask these people what they need from you in an unconditional, loving way. (*Pause.*)

Pay attention to any images or words, thoughts or feelings that may come up as you visualize this. Tell the people in front of you, what you need to receive, unconditionally, from them. Let the answers drift into your heart and mind, being aware of how you are reacting to these sensations. (*Pause.*)

If you do not receive an answer, that's O.K., it will come to you in a different way or at a different time.

Continue to experience the feelings of unconditional love. Tell yourself that you deserve to be given to by others and you are able to receive this beautiful love for yourself. Visualize your body covered in pink light, unconditional "love light." Feel the warmth and peace that is now covering your entire body. Allow the energies to stay with you for a few minutes.

Feel your Guides and Angels holding you in gentle peace and beautiful love as your Heart Chakra begins to open completely. Sit with this energy for as long as you like, breathing out any discomfort and knowing you are safe and protected. (*Pause.*)

When you are ready, thank your Angels and Guides for assisting you in this meditation. Invite them to go back to their own Realm in love and light. Know that at any time you may connect with them again. (*Pause.*)

Visualize a bright, strong gold bubble of light around your outer body. Feel its strength protecting you and holding you safe as you become aware of your surroundings. Feel the floor or chair beneath you. Become aware of your fingers and toes. Become aware of your breath and the pulse of the blood in your body. Allow all of your senses to return to the here and now. (*Pause.*)

When you are ready, open your eyes and log all your reactions, thoughts, and feelings in your journal. Bag and label the Fourth Chakra Incense and then take a few moments to sit with yourself and relax in the loving energy you created.

You are a lovable individual! You completely deserve unconditional love at all times in all ways.

You may have feelings of depression or elation after completing this meditation. If you feel sadness, let yourself cry. If you are feeling joy, allow yourself the freedom to embrace that joy. Own your feelings!

Let the energies of your wide-open heart chakra guide you in feeling all those previously blocked feelings. Allow yourself the magnificent experience of radiating love for others and for your self. Don't hold it back. Let it flow!

CHAPTER 14

Fifth Chakra –
Incense & Meditation

HERBS YOU WILL NEED:

- ½ cup Spearmint – Clears the lungs and the nasal passages, cleanses the fifth chakra.
- ¼ cup Frankincense – Raises vibrations in the body, clears negativity, opens the upper chakras.
- ½ cup Caraway Seeds – *Do Not Grind!* Clears out negative thoughts, aids in memory and communication.
- ¼ cup Benzoin Gum – Binder

OILS YOU WILL NEED:

- 10 drops Lemon oil – Clears the aura, aids in speaking to people.
- 6 drops Blue Food Coloring (optional)

Before you begin mixing Fifth Chakra Incense, close your eyes for a moment, inhale lightly through your nose and out through your mouth. Relax your mind. Now take a moment to relax your body. Roll your neck slowly, shrug your shoulders and stretch up above your heads and then reach for the floor. Hang forward, arms outstretched opening up the spine and the shoulders, relaxing the neck.

In our culture we are not always given the opportunity to speak the words we need to say to honor ourselves. That includes negative, as well as positive words. Sometimes we have to hold back our feelings from our bosses, loved ones or someone who has hurt us.

Fifth Chakra Incense is a tool to help release those pent up, unspoken words. It can be used in a meditative state although I prefer to speak while burning it, letting those words flow in a safe, loving place of solitude. Do what feels appropriate for you in this mixing.

Spearmint is the main ingredient for this Incense. It opens the throat, clears the nasal passages and adds "zip" to your energy centers. Feel the Spearmint as you place it in the mixing bowl. Smell it, letting the aroma connect to your body.

Add the other dried herbs, paying attention to how your throat and nasal passages are reacting as you create this mixture. (Sometimes this incense will create a sore throat or give you a slight sinus headache when you begin. Run some white light into those areas to clear the blockages or pain.)

Add the oils, again paying attention to how your body is reacting, especially in the throat and head. Do you want to chatter and make noise? Do you feel like stopping and calling your friends? Do you feel your throat constricting or loosening up as you mixed the herbs? Are you coughing or clearing your throat while mixing the recipe. Do you have a headache or sinus pressure? Do your ears hurt or ring while you are mixing? Pay attention to all those feelings and take time right now to log them in your journal.

Fifth Chakra Meditation

ITEMS YOU WILL NEED:

- Blue candle.
- Fifth Chakra incense.
- Charcoal briquette.
- Incense Burner.
- A mirror to stand or sit in front of.
- A glass of water or beverage.

Find a comfortable place to sit or stand. I prefer to stand for this speaking meditation, only because I feel more energy movement and better control of my breath when I stand. I leave it up to you and your comfort. I also prefer to do this exercise without music. I leave that to your preference also. Let's begin.

Take a few deep cleansing breaths, in through the nose and out through the mouth. Now inhale a deep breath of blue light in, hold it briefly then blow out blue through your mouth. You may find yourself coughing, choking and feeling more spittle in your mouth...all of these reactions are normal. Breathe in several more deep breaths of blue light, sending it into your throat area.

Get comfortable with the energy of the Fifth Chakra. Look at yourself in the mirror in front of you. If you feel uncomfortable, let those feelings come up. Think about all the things that you haven't said to yourself or to others that you feel need to be said. Feel free to express these things out loud. If you are doing this in a group meditation, just visualize it. Imagine the words propelling out of your throat and out of your mouth. See those words being circled in pink, loving light, like bubbles around the words.

This keeps negativity from flowing out into the Universe,
but also clears your system of negative thoughts and words.

After you have expressed all the words that need to flow out of you, take another deep breath of blue light, and release the breath. Think about all the good things you haven't heard people say to you lately. Say those things to yourself. Tell yourself that you are valuable. You are a lovable, wonderful human being and you deserve the best this life has to offer. Tell yourself that you are your very own best friend. Feel your throat choke up or relax as you do this. Pay attention to any pain you are experiencing in the body and breathe it out.

If you are having a negative response to these words, you may want to
look at what is creating the sense of not "deserving" all of these positive
thoughts.

Take another deep breath of blue light sending it into your throat area. Think about the various people that you may not have said positive things to lately. Express or visualize those thoughts now, feeling the energy of those positive words moving through your throat area and up and out through your mouth. Let yourself get comfortable with saying positive reinforcing words to others. Say those very positive statements to yourself as well. *(Pause.)*

When you feel like you are all "talked out," give yourself a mental hug and tell yourself you are deeply loved. Tell yourself that your words and feelings are valuable. Reinforce in your mind and your body that you are allowed to be expressive in your communications in everyday life.

Tell yourself that open communication with loved ones is acceptable and you have every right to express who you are and to feel passionate about your words and your feelings.

Reinforce in your heart, mind, body and Soul that your communication with God/Goddess/Spirit is acceptable and honored as well. Pause for a moment and quietly sit with that energy, letting yourself hear the words in your head and breathing through any pain or discomfort you may be feeling throughout your body.

Gently begin to come back to the here and now, wiggling your toes and fingers, feeling your throat relaxing and becoming aware of your current surroundings. Feel the floor beneath your feet and take a deep breath of white light in through your nose sending it down through your entire body and clearing your energy field.

Drink some of the water or beverage you brought into the room with you, feeling the liquid soothing your throat. Look at yourself in the mirror and tell yourself out loud " I did a great job of expressing who I am today and I will continue to express myself in everything I do and honor the feelings that come up with that expression."

Log your reactions and feelings during this meditation.

CHAPTER 15

Sixth Chakra Incense

HERBS YOU WILL NEED:

- ½ cup Rose Petals – Calls in Angels and Guides. Creates feelings of love.
- ½ cup Bay Leaves – Stimulates the crown chakra and third eye.
- ½ cup Eyebright – Increases clarity in the mind and opens the sixth chakra.
- ½ cup Star Anise – Magnetizes intuitive powers.
- ½ cup Lemon Peel – Heightens feelings of love.

OILS YOU WILL NEED:

- 5 drops Sandalwood oil – Soothes the nervous system, creates balance in the body.
- 5 drops Lemongrass oil – Clears the third eye, increases intuition.
- 5 drops Blue and red food coloring to create Indigo (optional)

Before you begin mixing these herbs I must give you some warning about this particular Incense. Sixth Chakra Incense is perhaps one of the strongest mixtures in this book. It produces a sudden elevation in psychic energy.

Before you begin mixing, you might want to protect your energy so you can focus on the blending until the time you are ready to do the energy work and meditation. Take a deep breath of gold light in through your nose and send it down through your body, then bring it up around you like a giant sleeping bag of protection. This will keep your Aura safe, your chakras protected and your energy a bit more grounded. If at any time during mixing you feel light-headed or over-sensitive, sit for a few moments and touch the floor with the palms of your hands.

Sixth Chakra Incense is a tool to move the blocks out of your higher psychic centers. The Sixth Chakra is located just above the eyebrows in the middle of the forehead. It governs the decision making process, psychic awareness and the ability to see through situations. Most people use this center for decision making.

As children, we used our Sixth Chakra to measure our psychic impressions. As we are growing and spending time in school, we are taught to pay more attention to our intellect than to our emotions and psychic abilities. I would like to wake that lost energy up in you and reconnect your body to the gift of second sight.

Mix the herbs together, paying attention to the way your body feels as you experience the energies of these herbs. If you develop a headache between the eyes, breathe in white light and send it to the sixth chakra. When you are done mixing the dried herbs, add the Lemongrass and Sandalwood oil. Pay attention to how you are feeling while mixing the recipe.

Do you have pressure in your forehead? Did you get a headache in your temples? Do you feel sensitive in your body while mixing this recipe? Does your body feel tingly or unusual? Do you feel "spacey" or "lightheaded?" Log these reactions in your journal and be specific, also log any substitutions you may have made in the recipe.

CHAPTER 16

Seventh Chakra Incense

HERBS YOU WILL NEED:

- ¼ cup Bay leaves – Heightens intuition and attunes the sixth chakra.
- ¼ cup Juniper – Rejuvenates energy, clears sacred space.
- ¼ cup Angelica – Blows the crown chakra open, raises intuition.
- ½ cup Rose Petals – Attracts Guides and Angels, opens the heart chakra.
- ¼ cup Benzoin Gum - Binder

OILS YOU WILL NEED:

- 5 drops Clove oil – Purifies the aura.
- 3 tsps. Honey – Calls in Angels.

Seventh Chakra Incense will open up the energy center at the top of your head... the Crown Chakra.

This center connects you to your personal Power and to the Higher Power/God/ Goddess/Spirit/Universe. It is a "hot line" to the Angelic realm, allowing input from your Guides, Angels and the Higher Self to come through.

When we pray, the Crown opens, and the Sixth Chakra, also known as the Third Eye, opens as well creating a 'psychic beacon'. We communicate with these higher energies on a daily basis, sometimes not even realizing we are doing it.

Occasionally, opening this area will create discomfort throughout the body. You might experience feeling "light headed," spacey, or disoriented. That's O.K. because that is the desired response. Just sit and ground when you feel too uncomfortable, breathe in some gold light to protect your energy while you are mixing and continue on, allowing the energy fluctuations to happen in your body so you can raise your personal energy vibrations.

Here we go now with Seventh Chakra Incense. Mix the dried herbs together. Feel your body reacting, becoming lighter, almost feathery. Add the Clove oil, paying attention to the smell. Clove oil is designed to clear the Aura of negativity and raise your vibrations. Honey calls out to your Angels and establishes connection to the Higher Power.

Really pay attention to any aches, pains and weird body feelings you may be experiencing or messages you are receiving in your head as you mix the recipe. Add the flower petals letting the roses continue to open your heart center and connect you to the Angelic Realm.

Pay attention again to how you feel, noticing how the room has filled up with energies other than your own. Feel the sensations that are now running up and down your body creating hot and cold vibrations in your physical body. Pay attention to the "buzziness" you may be feeling in your Crown Chakra.

Let all of it happen.

Log the experiences in your journal, being specific about how you are feeling.

Sixth And Seventh Chakra Meditation

YOU WILL NEED:

- A purple candle
- A white candle
- Two candle holders
- Sixth and Seventh Chakra Incense
- Charcoal briquette
- Incense holder
- Meditation music. It is helpful to record this meditation before you begin to meditate.

Find a comfortable place to meditate, either sitting on the floor or in a comfortable chair. Laying down for this meditation is also acceptable. Many of my students fell asleep the first time they practiced this meditation. They felt like they had traveled out of their bodies into an altered state of awareness. Let it happen. Don't doubt the sensations or question the experience.

Light the white candle and then the purple candle. Light the charcoal and place it in the burner letting it get hot. Take a few deep cleansing breaths in through your nose and out through your mouth. Send any stiffness in your body out of you with every release of breath, allowing your body to fully relax as you breathe in and out. Now put a pinch of Sixth and Seventh Chakra Incense on the charcoal.

Inhale purple light in through your nose and send it up to the Third Eye, in the center of your forehead. Let that light move around in the Sixth Chakra. Feel the sensations your body is experiencing as you do this. If you have any discomfort, blow the pain or anxiety out through your mouth. (*Pause.*)

As the energy of purple light moves around your Sixth Chakra, ask your Guides and Angels to come to you. Ask them to protect you as you open up your psychic centers to reach your "Higher Self."

> *Your Higher self is that voice that resounds through your body when you are in an off-balance or fearful state. It's the knowing that says you should or should not experience this.*

Take another gentle, deep breath of purple light sending it again to your Sixth Chakra. Feel the energy moving in circles around your forehead. Feel your senses opening up to that magnificent, vibrant energy. (*Pause here.*)

Now send purple light up into the top of your head and out of the Crown Chakra. Feel it releasing. Your Sixth Chakra is still open and aligning with your body's energy. Ask for your Guides and Angels to come in stronger and assist you in this process. (*Pause.*)

Visualize white light streaming from spirit, the Universal Life Force into the top of your head. Take deep, cleansing breaths as you feel the energy of the Universe fill your body. Let the white light circle the top of your head. See white light moving through your face and down through your neck. (*Pause.*)

Let the white light flow into your heart chakra. Let it move into your stomach area. Let the energy move further down into your pelvis. Rest with it a moment. Gently send the white light into your legs. Now move that beautiful white light into your feet. Take a gentle deep breath and send the white light through your toes and out your body into the floor. (*Pause.*)

Bring your attention to your Aura. Visualize brilliant white light radiating around your Aura, clearing any energy blocks you may have. Sit with this energy for a while, relaxing into the comfort of Universal Light Energy. (*Pause.*)

Gently ask your Guides and Angels to come to you for a third time. Visualize them all around you in love and light. You are completely protected. You are one with them at this time. (*Pause.*)

Take a deep breath and ask them to give you information about your path. Are you on the right path? *(Pause.)*

What do you need to look at to clear any blocks to your current path? (Pause)

What healing do you need to work on and what prevents you from using your psychic energy and perhaps healing talents to the fullest? (Pause here.)

Pay attention to the answers, images, feelings that are coming up for you right now. Let them flow through you and around you, accepting the messages the Universe is attempting to share with you.

Take a deep breath in and ask the Universe/Spirit/God/Goddess what your divine purpose is and what you need to do to achieve that? *(Pause.)*

When you feel like you are finished conversing with your Guides and Angels, thank them for visiting with you and protecting you. Know that they are with you always and will speak to you at any time. Ask them to help you keep your Third Eye and Crown Chakra open to receive more messages in the future. *(Pause.)*

Now inhale deeply and visualize the Universal white light and the purple light of your Sixth Chakra staying with you. See droplets of gold light falling gently around your shoulders and head. Let those droplets of pure, protective energy fall around your entire body, encasing you in a bubble of gold. *(Pause here.)*

Slowly become aware of your body touching the ground. Wiggle your toes, your fingers and move your arms and legs slowly. Feel the sensations of the room around you. Become aware of the smells in the room, the sounds and the strength of your own breath going in and out.

When you are ready, open your eyes and come back to the present time, allowing your body to wake up and stretch itself back to life.

You may have a "spacey" feeling after this meditation, so take some time to ground your energy. Eat some chocolate or protein, touch the floor with your palms and drink some water. This meditation and both Incenses' will heighten your sensitivity. If you have to go out in the world after completing this meditation, continue to put gold light around yourself to keep your intuitive centers protected.

If you came out of the meditation with a headache or dull throbbing in your forehead, breathe in gold light and send it to the pain. Visualize the Third Eye closing gently. Imagine a real eye in the middle of your forehead. See that eye gently closing, but not all the way, relieving the pressure of opening your psychic center too much. This should alleviate any pain.

Congratulations! You have blown open your Chakras and manifested some fantastic healing in your own life, as well as others! Treat yourself to a sea salt bath. Buy yourself a bouquet of gorgeous flowers or treat yourself to a box of your favorite chocolates for completing the work thus far.

You now shine brighter from the inside out than when you first began creating the recipes in this manual. Be proud of yourself for going through the process. I am proud of you as well!

CHAPTER 17

Etheric Incense

ONE DAY, in the back room of my office where most of my incense was created, me and my daughter Melissa, were happily mixing up the recipes in this book to use in my healing practice. As we mixed the Eighth Chakra Incense, Melissa completely stopped what she was doing. Her little ten-year old face looked very quizzical at me, as she tilted her head to the side and asked, "Mommy, what frequency do you think Jesus and Buddha worked on? I think they must have had a very large Aura to do the things they did. I think they expanded their energy to a higher level."

I stopped mixing the incense and stared at her beautiful sky-blue eyes. I wondered to myself, "How old are you really?" I couldn't really tell her what frequency the Masters might have worked on since I had not been in their living energies. The entire time we worked I pondered her question, while we finished mixing the incense recipes.

A few hours later, after many of the recipes were created, Melissa came to me with a crumpled up piece of paper. On it was the recipe for Etheric Incense. I was stunned. I asked her how she knew what to put in it. She shrugged her shoulders and replied, "My Angels told me."

As you mix this incense, be aware of your Guides and Angels around you. This mixture definitely attracts them! This incense will also expand your Aura and attract people to you for healing. My little shop overflowed with clients and customers as soon as we started mixing the herbs together and added the oils.

Customers wanted more information about healing, angels, psychics; it was like a blue light special on energy as they flocked in to see us. We happily worked with them, forgetting to test the Etheric incense Melissa had created from her angel's messages. We didn't have to test it; it did its work while sitting raw in the incense bowl of our back room.

HERBS YOU WILL NEED:

- ¼ cup Peppermint – Heightens intuition and connection to Spirit.
- ⅛ cup Chamomile – Caresses the heart chakra and promotes feelings of peacefulness.
- ⅛ cup Jasmine – Harmonizes the body.
  ¼ cup Orange Peel – Creates feelings of love and bliss.
- ⅛ cup Sesame Seeds – Opens the base and second chakra
- ⅛ cup Benzoin Powder – Binder

OILS YOU WILL NEED:

- 5 drops Penny Royal – Inspires feelings of peace.
- 5 drops Hyacinth – Stimulates the heart chakra to share love.
- 5 drops Pine – Increases abundance.
- 5 drops Yellow or green food coloring (optional)

Mix all the herbs together. Pay attention to the aroma coming off each one. Let the smell resonate to your own energy centers. Pay attention to your skin. You will feel a tingling sensation occurring as your Aura begins to feel the aroma and respond to it. Do not be alarmed, it's supposed to happen. Mix in the oils carefully. Do these very slowly so you can move into a much higher energy level without becoming disoriented or sick.

Let your body shift and move with the energy of this incense. If you feel like dancing or singing go ahead. This mixture tends to give the user a sense of elation and peace. When you smell the finished incense, visualize healing energy going out to others much like the Reiki exercise. Picture yourself as a conductor for healing those around you, knowing that you are protected at all times from negativity.

Ask for the Master teachers to assist you in charging this incense for the highest good of all mankind. Feel the radiance of their energy flow through your body and down into the Aura Incense. Breathe deeply as you feel the energies of Jesus, Buddha, Usui, Yogananda Paramahansa, Ghandi, and the Mother Mary, Universal Light Healers, and the Gods and Goddesses from every Realm. (*Pause.*)

Feel the top of your head buzzing and your skin feeling electric as you become even more aware of the Master healers that have filled the room you are in. Let those energies continue to work around you, filling you up with their wisdom, unconditional love and divine energies. Breathe in and out as you let those radiant energies assimilate together. (*Pause.*)

Let yourself float in this energy for as long as you like, grounding yourself when you are finished. Be sure to drink plenty of water afterwards to re-hydrate. Know that you can call on this energy at any time with or without this particular incense, it is only a tool to boost your natural energy.

Record the sensations you experienced in your journal. Record any messages you received from the Master Healers, any visions you might have seen or emotions that filtered up while you floated with the Masters. Enjoy the day and make sure you honor the people who will come in around you to enjoy the energy you are radiating.

Your aura is shining and pulsing for everyone to see. Protect it if you need to with gold light.

CHAPTER 18

Favorite Recipes

THE LAST CHAPTER of this book contains some of my favorite incense recipes. Most of these recipes were specifically designed for individuals who frequented the store I volunteered in. They are powerful, fun and can create positive change in your life.

I have done short meditations after creating these incense recipes, but most of the time I use them to change the vibrations in the space I am in. I enjoy using the recipes when I need an energetic lift, or when I need to calm down to meditate. I'm sure whatever the need you will find good uses for these varieties.

I did, however, log my feelings and experiences when I made these recipes, because just like the previous mixtures, these too will cause you to process.

Seasonal Recipes

Yule Incense

This Incense was created for the celebration of the Winter Solstice. I burn it to lighten up my house and get myself in the mood for sharing, receiving unconditional gifts, to attract money and to honor the energies of the dying earth.

On the Solstice, December 21st, my family did a meditation asking for world peace, harmony in our household, and prosperity for the coming year. We burned the Yule Incense and had everyone hold a lit white candle. It is now a tradition that we have incorporated into our home.

We stood in a circle and offered up healing energy, and prayers for those we loved and for the planet. It was better than any gift we could have received and now it is part of our holiday celebrations.

HERBS YOU WILL NEED:

- 3 Bay Leaves – Opens the crown chakra to feel Spirit. Attracts prosperity and goodwill.
- ½ cup Orange Peel – Clears the second chakra, creating joy and creativity.
- ¼ cup ground Nutmeg – Attracts wealth and abundance.
- ¼ cup Cinnamon chips – Raises energy in the body, clears negativity and stimulates the mind.
- ⅛ cup Cloves ground – Clears negativity, creates creativity and inspires joy.
- ¼ cup Frankincense – Purifies sacred space while magnifying the body's energy. Attracts abundance and peace.
- ¼ cup Myrrh – Aids in healing the body, purifying sacred space and increasing intuition.

OILS YOU WILL NEED:

- 5 drops Pine oil – Increases prosperity and cleanses the aura.
- 5 drops Clove oil – Attracts opportunities and wealth.
- 10 drops Green Food Coloring (optional)

Yule Incense can be mixed as incense or potpourri.
If you mix it as a potpourri, eliminate the frankincense and myrrh.
You can add pinecones, dried apples, dried oranges and
spiced rose hips.

Spring Incense

During the months of January and February, when the Earth is sleeping and the ground is usually white, I enjoy buying aromatic, fresh flowers. I bring them home, admire their beauty, let them wilt, and hang them from the beams in my South Carolina home.

I package the dried leaves, stems and flowers to use for Spring Incense and any other recipes that call for dried flowers. Simply tie a rubber band or ribbon around the end of the stem and hang the flowers upside down from a rod. I use an old tree branch I brought in from outdoors that a great old Oak donated to me for this very purpose.

When the flowers are dried, you can clean off all the usable parts, depending on what kind of flowers you are drying, and package them up for later use in incense and potpourris'.

HERBS YOU WILL NEED:

- ¼ cup Hibiscus – Elevates feelings of love and intuitive knowing.
- ½ cup Rose petals or Rose Hips – Calls in Angels and Spirits. Inspires feelings of love.
- ⅛ cup Patchouli – Instills feelings of love and earthiness. Attracts abundance. Opens the heart chakra.
- ¼ cup White Willow Bark – Attracts love and joy.
- ⅛ cup Marjoram – Raises feelings of happiness and love.
- ⅛ cup Benzoin Gum – Binds and strengthens the mixture.

OILS YOU WILL NEED:

- 5 drops Rose oil – Attracts the Angelic realm and opens the heart to love.
- 3 drops Patchouli oil – Increases feelings of love and sexuality. Attracts wealth.

Test this incense for the strength of the oils as you add them. Sometimes the Marjoram and Patchouli can be very strong. You will want to "mask" these aromas with the Rose oil.

This particular incense can be used to stuff sachet bags and dream pillows with. Leave out the Benzoin Gum and add five extra drops of rose oil to the mixture to enhance the scent.

Enjoy the springtime!

Animal Recipes

Totem Incense

Elizabeth, a really good friend of mine was doing a lot of soul searching, and looking for her spiritual path. She asked me if I could create some animal incense recipes to help her connect with her Totems. (Animal spirits.) She believed, as I do, that everyone has animal guides that teach us, just like Angels or loved ones who have passed on.

I thought long and hard about how I would go about creating the incense that would bring in her Totems. I studied real animals and mythical animals, logging their attributes and cross-referencing what herbs would match those attributes. Below is the incense that did just that for her.

You can create your own special kind of animal incense to align with creatures that appeal to you. If you cannot find a specific herb that will work in the pages of this book, meditate on it for a few minutes.

Eventually a specific herb will speak to your subconscious and you will have discovered the right mixture to create your own Totem incense. Below are a few of the recipes created for Elizabeth and others searching for the connection to their Totems.

Dolphin Incense

HERBS YOU WILL NEED:

- ½ cup Balm of Gilead – Creates an open heart and feelings of self love.
- ¼ cup Jasmine – Works on the second chakra, creating feelings of passion and connection. Dispels depression and stress.
- ½ cup Marshmallow – Increases feelings of being connected to loved ones and of being loved by others. Inspires the fourth chakra to open.
- ¼ cup Violet flowers – Create feelings of love and connection in the first and second chakras. Opens the body up to giving and receiving unconditional love.
- ¼ cup Sandalwood – Stimulates the seventh chakra, creates sensitivity in the body and creates clarity in the mind.

OILS YOU WILL NEED:

- 5 drops Violet oil – Healing and soothing. Calms the nervous system and opens the heart up for love.

Dolphin Incense connects you to your past lives. It can also connect you to your *knowing* about other people. Breathe in the smoke as you meditate on who you might have been in a previous existence or what you need to see in the people around you.

Become in-tune with that "old self" from long ago. Look at what knowledge or lessons you brought back into this lifetime. Acknowledge the things that are coming up about the people you are questioning. Thank Dolphin for speaking to you and log your experiences.

Dragon Incense

HERBS YOU WILL NEED:

- ½ cup Allspice – Opens the base chakra, raising vibrations in the body. Attracts, luck, money and inspires strength.
- ½ cup Ash bark- ground – Heightens positive feelings and power. Opens the third chakra, energizing and opening the body up to "old wisdom."
- 1 root Galangal ground – Opens the third eye and increases intuitive perception. Attracts abundance in all forms and protects, cleanses and purifies the home. (Ginger is an excellent substitution for Galangal).
- ¼ cup Rue – Opens the base chakra and is protective energetically.
- ⅛ cup Dragon's Blood Powder (made from ground Dragon's Blood Resin). – Magnifies energy in the body, adds potency to herbal mixtures.
- ⅛ cup Benzoin Gum – Binder.

OILS YOU WILL NEED:

- 3 drops Cinnamon oil- Raises spiritual vibrations, attracts wealth and clears negativity. (Caution! This oil will burn your skin if you get it on you... use with care).

I wanted to fly, soar and be passionate after I burned this incense. It creates very strong, aggressive feelings in people and animals, so use caution when burning it.

Meditate with this incense when you need the wisdom of dragon.
They are the record keepers of knowledge and strength.
Tap into Dragon's energy when you feel the need to increase
your passion, feel the heat of inspiration or the power of being,
protected by the greatest fire animal in history.

Owl Incense

HERBS YOU WILL NEED:

- ¼ cup Lavender – Soothes the nervous system, Opens the heart chakra and third eye. Purifies the body creating peace in the chakras.
- ¼ cup Cinnamon chips ground – Opens the base and heart chakra. Amplifies

intuition, raises energetic vibrations. Clears negativity and promotes healing in the body.

- ⅛ cup Eucalyptus – Opens the fifth chakra for heightened communication and emotional clarity.
- ⅛ cup Ginger – Opens the heart and the third chakra, instills feelings of power and love. Clears negative energy and raises vibrations in the body.
- ⅛ cup Sage – Clears sacred space and raises vibrations in the home.

OILS YOU WILL NEED:

- 7 drops Rose oil- Promotes thoughts of love, opens the heart chakra and invites the Angels and Guides in to speak with you.

Owl Incense connects the user with the wisdom and knowledge of Owl. It will allow messages from Spirit to come in and speak to you about your path. Pay attention to the messages you receive or the interaction with the spirit realm that may occur after using Owl incense.

You might notice Owls more prominently after meditating with this mixture. You might feel more intuitive or aware of the dead trying to speak to you. Your dreams may bring in messages from loved ones and those that have crossed over. Pay attention as Owl flies into your energy and brings you the messages of the night.

Owls are the keeper of spirit messages and will bring you insight into their world.

Conclusion

I HOPE you have enjoyed this book, the gifts it may have brought you, and all the processing I know you may have gone through in order to create the recipes given here. My wish in creating *Scents of the Soul* was to open you up to the Universe and all the healing it has to offer you on every level.

My goal was to give you the tools to connect your energy with that of your Angels and Guides. I hope you had the opportunity to meet them, hear them and become aware of their presence in your life..

My deepest wish for you is that you continue to experience delightful, enlightening, healing journeys full of love and harmony throughout your lifetime. May the blessings of the Universe bring Divine Peace into your life.

May the healing energy of Herbs, and all of their powerful attributes bring you closer to the sweet aroma of your unique, beautiful Soul.

Candle Colors & Correspondences

BLACK: Black absorbs all light with little or no reflection back, thus it becomes a receptacle or a transporter in energy work and healing. Use in meditation to absorb and release negativity. It breaks up stagnant energy. It represents wisdom, and the unconscious.

BROWN: Brown represents earth energy, grounding, legal matters and weight. Brown assists in intuitively locating lost objects and improving powers of concentration and telepathy. It is a protection color for household pets, grounding and centering your consciousness with the earth. Visualize brown to attune with trees.

GOLD: The male half of the Cosmic or Universal life force, God-sun energy. Gold represents intelligent action, deliberation and knowledge. It is used for healing and protection. When Visualized, Gold attracts wealth and abundance. It aligns with the power of cosmic influences.

GRAY: It is a perfect balance of black and white, and therefore absorbs and repels energy. Gray draws in undesirable energies and then sends them out to the universe for dispersal into light energy.

Use to erase, cancel, neutralize, and return unwanted energies to the Universe. Be cautious with the color Gray for it will either attract constructive or destructive energies to your life (this includes people and situations).

GREEN: Green stimulates growth, plant life and unconditional love. Green attracts money and if meditated on with a specific amount in mind, it will aid in manifesting it quickly.

Visualize green to attract success, good luck, prosperity, money, rejuvenation, ambition and fertility. Green aids in communicating with plants or fairies and stimulates growth in the garden when visualized flowing through and around the plants.

ORANGE: Orange is a combination of yellow and red. Yellow is mental energy and red is active energy. When combined the color orange is created, also creating activity in the body and mind. Visualize orange to attract prosperity and nurture your energy. Orange attracts others in a positive way to your life.

Meditating on the color orange attracts, success, good luck and fortune. Orange represents vitality and stamina while encouraging fun and discouraging laziness.

PINK: Pink is a lighter shade of red. It deals with spiritual, emotional love rather than the physical form. Pink represents unconditional love that flows out from the heart and is freely shared without restrictions or expectations. It is the color of friendship and nurturing.

Pink raises vibrations, increases selfless love, heightens feminine energy and amplifies spiritual healing. Visualize Pink to release feelings of selfishness and loneliness.

PURPLE: Purple is the color of expansion in all forms, and expands anything you desire. Meditate with Purple to expand spirituality, business, money, health or love. Purple brings more of what you already have and attracts wisdom, high idealism, and knowledge of the higher spiritual realms. It represents spiritual protection, healing, and your highest potential. Purple also represents power, psychic ability, male energy, protective energy and recognition in your chosen field.

RED: Use the lighter, brighter shades of red to enhance lust, physical desire and movement. Leave the darker shades alone. The darker shades are for wars, battles, hate and danger. Red magnetizes feelings of anger, hate, survival and confrontation. Red is the color of war, and attracts, magnetizes and promotes courage. Red stimulates and energizes.

WHITE: Is a combination of all colors and reflects light with little to no absorption. It represents the most highly balanced form of spirituality possible. White contains virtues in their highest form, and is therefore very protective. It is beyond the word or term God/Goddess. It is the Creative Source itself, zero, the alpha, the light from which all life springs, the female aspect of God, the symbol of the life giving Mother and all female mysteries.

Use White candles for consecration rituals, meditation, divination, and all work that involves healing, clairvoyance, truth, peace and spiritual strength. White is also used to contact guides and angels, and balance the Aura.

YELLOW: Yellow is the color of mental clarity, swiftness and accuracy. Meditate on yellow to obtain knowledge, retain information and gain insight into problems. It represents all institutions of learning and science, while enhancing knowledge of healing, the ability to concentrate and retention of memory. Wearing yellow also attracts people.

BLUE: Blue is a neutral color and applies equally to female and male energies. Blue promotes calmness, tranquility, written and oral skills, sleep, peace, loyalty, good-will, purification, protection, hope, sincerity, mature love and commitment, truth, patience, guidance and freedom. Meditate on Blue to speak your mind, heal the body and clear out feelings of anger.

SILVER: Silver represents female energy and has similar qualities to white. It is the color for purity, protection, ice, stars, potential and fame. Use silver for divination, clairvoyance, energy, inspiration, defense and repelling negative energy. Meditate on silver to connect the Goddess self, emotions and the energies of the Full Moon.

Meditation Music

- *Atlantis Healing Temple*, Robert Slap 1-818-889-1575 Beautiful zone out music! My favorite.
- *Chakra Healing Zone*, David and Steve Gordon with Sequoia Artists. www.sequoiarecords.com
- *Fairy Lullabies*, Gary Stadler www.sequoiarecords.com
  An enchanting, soothing compilation of instrumental lullabies that will connect you to your fairy guides and delight your inner child.
- *Lesiem*, Intentcity Records,1-714-630-0209 (Enigma meets Pink Floyd)
- *Reiki Harmony*, Terry Oldfield. Available through New Earth Records 1-800-570-4074.
- *Sound Massage*, Dean Evenson & Soundings Ensemble. Available through www.soundings.com or 1-800-93-PEACE.
- *Tribal Winds, Music from Native American Flutes*, Earthbeat Records 1-800-346-4445

Wholesale Suppliers

- www.driedflowersdirect.com Keuka Flower Farm 3597 Skyline Dr. Penn Yan, NY 14527 1 315-536-2736
- www.gaigarden.com Gaia Garden Herbals 2672 West Broadway, Vancouver BC, Canada V6K 2G3, 1-866-734-HERB (4372). Gaia has an outstanding reputation for seeds and plants.
- www.mountainroseherbs.com Mountain Rose Herbs PO Box 50220 Eugene OR 1-800–879-3337
- www.scentsofsuccess.com Scents of Success 1-800-580-5579 Supplies hard-to-find essential oils such as Rose, Oak Moss and Melissa.
- Spirit Dancer Sage P.O. Box 644, Sedona Arizona 86339 928-282-7536 Supplier of smudge sticks, loose Sage, Resins and Charcoal.
- www.twoguysspice.com - Specialized store for dried spices and herbal mixtures.

Bibliography

- Aima: *Ritual Book of Herbal Spells.* – Los Angeles, Foibles, 1976.
- Agrippa, Henry Cornelius: *Three Books of Occult Philosophy.* – 1533. London 1651. Reprint, London; Chthonios Books, 1986.
- Anodea, Judith: *Wheels of Life, A Users Guide to the Chakra System.* – Llewellyn, 1987.
- Arctander, Steffen: *Perfume and Flavor Materials of Natural Origin.* – Elizabeth, New Jersey, 1960.
- Baerheim, Svendson, Scheffer: *Essential Oils and Aromatic Plants.* – Dr. W. Junk, 1985.
- Baker, Margaret: *Gardner's Magic and Folklore.* – New York, Universe Books, 1978.
- Beyerl, Paul: *The Holy Book of the Devas: The Secret Mythologies of the Herbal World.* – The Hermit's Grove, 1998 (4th edition)
- Beyerl, Paul: *Master Book of Herbalism.* – Custer, WA; Phoenix Publishing, 1984.
- Buckland, Raymond: *Practical Candle Burning Rituals.* – St. Paul, MN., Llewellyn, 1970.
- Coffin, Tristam P. and Henning Cohen; *Folklore Namerica.* – Garden City, New York, Anchor Books, 1970.
- Cunningham, Scott: *Magical Herbalism.* – Llewellyn's Practical Magick Series, 1982.
  — *Encyclopedia of Magickal Herbs.* – St. Paul, Llewellyn Publications, 1988
  — *The Magic of Incense, Oils and Brews.* – St. Paul; Llewellyn Publications, 1988
- Duff, Gail: *A Book of Potpourri.* – New and Old Ideas for Fragrant Flowers and Herbs. New York, Beaufort Books 1985.

- Dunwich, Gerina: *Wicca Candle Magick.* – Kensington Publishing Corporation-1989
- *Candlelight Spells.* – Secaucus NJ, Citadel Press, 1988.
- Friend, Hilderic: *Flowerlore.* – London, 1884, Rocktop (Maine), Para Research, 1981.
- Graves, Robert: *The White Goddess.* – New York, Farrar, Straus & Groux, 1976.
- Grieve, M.: *A Modern Herbal.* – New York, 1931. New York, Dover, 1971.
- Gordon, Leslie: *A Country Herbal.* – New York, Mayflower, 1980.
- *Green Magic.* – New York, Viking Press, 1977
- Michael T. Murray: *The Healing Power of Herbs.* – Rocklin, CA, Prima Publishing, 1992
- Gordon- Gardener, Joy, Pocket Guide to Chakras, Berkeley, California, The Crossing Press 1998.
- Horan, Paula, *Ultimate Reiki Touch, Initiation and Self Exploration for Healing.* – 18-19 Dilshad Garden, G.T. Road, Delhi-110, 095-India, Full Circle, 1999.
- Ingerman, Sandra: *Soul Retrieval, Mending the Fragmented Self.* – New York, NY; Harper Collins, 1991.
- Leyel, C.F.: *The Magic of Herbs.* – New York; 1927 Toronto (Canada); Coles Publishing, 1981.
- Lust, John: *The Herb Book.* – New York; Bantam, 1974
- Maple, Eric: *The Magic of Perfume.* – New York, Weiser, 1973.
- Mark and Luebeck, Walter Hosak: *Big Book of Reiki Symbols.* – Shangri la, India, 2006.
- Meyer, David. Sachets: *Potpourri and Incense Recipes.* – Glenwood, Illinois; Meyerbooks, 1986.
- Moldenke, Harold N. and Alma L.: *Plants of the Bible.* – Waltham, MA; Chronica Botanica Company,1952.
- Pliny the Elder (Caius Plinius Seciendus): *Natural History.* – Cambridge, Harvard University Press, 1956.
- Pond, David: *Chakras for Beginners.* – St. Paul, Minn., Llewellyn, 2001.
- Riva, Anna: *The Modern Herbal Spell book.* – Toluca Lake, California, International Imports, 1974.
- Thistleton, Dyer, T.F.: *The Folklore of Plants.* – Detroit, Singing Tree Pines, 1968.
- Thompkins, Peter and Christopher Bird: *The Secret Life of Plants.* – New York: Avon Books, 1974.
- Usui, Dr. Mikao and Petter, Frank Arjava: *The Original Reiki Handbook.* – Box 325 Twin Lakes WI, Lotus Press, 2000

- Vinui, Leo: *Incense, Its Ritual Significance, Use and Preparation*. – New York, Weiser, 1980.
- Lubeck, Walter: *Complete Reiki Handbook*. – P.O. Box 325, Twin lakes, WI, Lotus Light Publications, 1994
- Worwood, V.A.: *Aromatics*. – Pan Books, London, 1987.
- Wheelwrite, Edith Grey: *Medicinal Plants and their History*. – New York, Dover Publications, New York, 1974.
- Wylundt: *Wylundt's Book of Incense*. – York Beach, ME; Samuel Weiser, 1989.

Dedications &
Acknowledgements

To my Dad – Joseph Hoage

YOU ALWAYS had a straw hat on your kind, balding head and ragged, leather gardening gloves on your large, gentle hands which covered your genius of a green thumb.

You were my loving guide to digging in the dirt, sprinkling crumbled flakes of Mica around my head and instilling in me the very essence of plant life. You taught me the art of hybridizing majestic Iris blooms and unique plant creations that bore the name of the people you loved.

You planted my little feet, deep in the cool earth to show me what trees felt like. You took me on adventurous rock hunts, introducing me to all the natural elements of the earth. You quietly woke me up in the middle of the night to accompany you to the back porch, pointing and gazing at the sequined night sky, silently searching for obscure planets and stars. You taught me to create beauty in every living thing I touched just like you did.

I love you Daddy.

To Sandy and Debbie

You were my loving Goddess mentors who taught me the fine art of being me. I offer up humble gratitude to the many teachers who have crossed paths with me. There have been many people along the way who have shared their brilliant wisdom in healing, herbs, essential oils, positive energy movement, and meditation.

Thank you to the literary teachers; Scott Cunningham, Steven R. Smiths, Dorothy Morrison, Gerald Gardner, and Raymond Buckland.

All my love and gratitude to my "Earth Angels" Mom and Dad, Debbie, Sandy, Kasey, Griff, Elizabeth, Heidi, David, and Morgan. Many thanks to Rob the computer fix-it guru, Nikki the earth mother, Suzette the Fairy Queen, Daughters of the Crystal Magnolia, Children of the Mystic Moon, and of course all the clients and students who have crossed my path over the years in my reading practice.

To my beloved husband Charles, you believed in every thought and word I wrote: thank you for being my cheerleader, inspiration and anchor in everything I do. You are magnificent in so many ways and I am truly blessed to have found you in this lifetime.

A grateful hug and kiss to James and Melissa, my two lovely children. You brought me macaroni and cheese on those long nights of writing about my latest hot bowl of incense... I love you more than that!

To the kind, enlightened wordsmiths at Findhorn Press, I thank you from the bottom of my heart for taking a chance on my work. Your guidance in the process of giving birth to the vision written on these pages has been a shimmering well of knowledge and caring.

Deep thanks to Sabine Weeke for reading my words and bringing me on board with Findhorn Press, gratitude to Damian Keenan for your inspirational cover art and illustrations and a warm Walt Disney wave to Michael Hawkins for giving my words a silver lining of beauty and grace. You are all appreciated more than words could ever express!

A thousand thanks to all the unnamed, unique individuals who enlightened me in the ways of mixing, stirring, creating, raising energy, meditating and being at peace with my own Soul. There are many who have touched my heart in ways they wouldn't begin to know... but I know and the gratitude and love is deep.

To both of the maternal figures in my life, Margaret and Sharon – your deep desire was to see me happy... I am.

FINDHORN PRESS

Books, Card Sets,
CDs & DVDs
that inspire and uplift

For a complete catalogue,
please contact:

Findhorn Press Ltd
305a The Park, Findhorn
Forres IV36 3TE
Scotland, UK

Telephone
+44-(0)1309-690582
Fax
+44-(0)131-777-2711
eMail
info@findhornpress.com

or consult our catalogue online
(with secure order facility) on
www.findhornpress.com

For information on the Findhorn Foundation:
www.findhorn.org